Reference and Information Services

This book may not be
removed from the library

London Borough of Camden
Libraries and Arts
Department

Windsurfing
Racing Technique

Philip Pudenz / Karl Messmer

Windsurfing Racing Technique

Photos by Michael Garff

STANFORD MARITIME
LONDON

Stanford Maritime Limited
Member Company of the George Philip Group
12–14 Long Acre   London WC2E 9LP
Editor Phoebe Mason

First published in Great Britain 1983
English edition © Stanford Maritime
and Buchheim Editions SA 1983

Translated into English by Barbara Webb

Originally published as *Regattatechnik Windsurfen*
© Buchheim Editions SA Fribourg 1983

Set in 11/12 Monophoto Univers by
Tameside Filmsetting Limited
Ashton-under-Lyne, Lancashire

Printed in West Germany by G. J. Manz Aktiengesellschaft, München

British Library Cataloguing in Publication Data

Pudenz, Philip
    Windsurfing racing technique.
    1. Windsurfing
    I. Title   II. Messmer, Karl
    III. Regattatechnik Windsurfen. *English*
    797.1'4   GV811.63.W56
ISBN 0-540-07415-2

CONTENTS

INTRODUCTION 7

TECHNIQUE 11

Tacking 13
Gybing 16
Starts 20
Closehauled Sailing 26
Reaching 30
Downwind Sailing 33
Rounding Marks 36
720° Turns 40
Trapeze Harness 42

COURSES, STARTS AND FLAG SIGNALS 45

The Olympic Course 46
Kiel Week Triangular Course 47
Timing and Flag Signals 47
Scoring Systems 47

TACTICS 51

Psychological Attitude 52
Dirty Wind and Blanketing 53

The Start 57
The First Beat 68
Reaching Legs 77
The Second Beat 86
The Downward Leg 86
The Final Beat, and Finishing the Race 90

EQUIPMENT 93

Theory of sails 93

Aerodynamics 94—Pressure and Force 94— Forces on the Sail and Board 95—Sail Fullness 97—
Mylar vs Dacron/Terylene 99—Mast and Sail as a Unit 101—Profile Shape 102

Tuning Tips 103

OTHER COMPETITION CLASSES 113

Funboards 113
Tandem Class 128
Speed Sailing 139
'Ins and Outs' and Slalom Racing 148

IYRU RACING RULES 149
BOARD CONSTRUCTION RULES 152

Division I Flat Boards 153
Division II Open Class 158
Division III Tandems 162

INTRODUCTION

The fleet before the start

The moment that someone finds he can actually stand up on his sailboard, the urge to compete is sure to surface, even if that just means seeing if he can stay up longer, tack quicker or gybe better than someone else.

The time is bound to come, however, when the most important question is 'who can sail faster?'

Competition is not restricted merely to racing round a course; there are many other ways of assessing how well you perform. Pleasure can be found in defeat as well as in winning, because in both cases competing at

On Sylt, a North Sea island where long beaches and breaking waves have made it a famous winsurfing centre

any level gives an indication of your skill and limitations, and a feeling of satisfaction if you have sailed well in terms of your level of ability. It is always easiest to judge your skill by comparing it to that of others.

Every windsurfer's ambition is to sail as well as possible and to continue to improve, whether the competition is in formal racing or in seeing who is fastest to cross some estuary.

This book can aid an advanced windsurfer to achieve his goal. The information, hints and advice in the sections on 'Technique' and 'Tactics' should help anyone to improve his skills. Technique, the subject of the first chapter, must be the first concern, both for the experienced sailor and for the person who is keen to race. Optimum board handling in every conceiveable

Cort Larned sailing in a force 6 wind at a funboard regatta

situation is an essential requirement: without it, it is much more difficult, if not quite impossible, to use tactics successfully.

There is a limit to the amount of concentration that anyone has at his disposal. When racing, technique should require the minimum of attention so that problems relating to tactics can be dealt with more effectively. Even the best windsurfer was once a beginner and knows that when your technique is poor and you fear you may fall off the board, you never have a spare moment to consider how to get into the front row at the start, which end of the starting line is better, or which tack to choose after crossing the line.

The illusion that good sailors are born that way dies hard, but just as perfect technique can be learned, so can tactics. This book gives basic examples which can be practised as easily as one can practise efficient gybing. Experience has proved that a sailor with sound technique and tactical knowledge can start a race feeling considerably more relaxed and self-confident.

Tandem boards are another challenge for the sailor who has progressed beyond the basic board-handling skills. They demand somewhat different techniques, however, and these are demonstrated here by experts.

The matter of equipment, and the different types of competition, are discussed later on in the book, and finally there is a section concerning the international board measurement and Division rules, and some of the IYRU Racing Rules that are particularly relevant to windsurfing.

TECHNIQUE

*Windsurfers camping on the beach. Important
championships are often held in warm sunny places*

In terms of training theory, the first goal in most
sports is perfect technique, and windsurfing is no
exception. Training to increase endurance, strength
and speed is useless unless it is linked to the training of
technical skills. When you improve your technique the
result is that your endurance increases because you
expend less energy; learning to tack and gybe perfectly
has the same effect. Furthermore, good technique
means being able to perform well without thinking
about it, and even when tired. This allows you to
concentrate on the racing situation.

In this chapter manoeuvring and the various points
of sailing are considered in depth so as to provide the
basic expertise needed to improve further.

Tacking

Every sailor has to learn to tack, that is to alter course by turning the *bow* through the wind while moving from one side of the sail to the other.

The first method of tacking could be called the **safe tack**: turn the board slowly onto the opposite tack with your feet while holding the rig with the uphaul line to the side to which you are turning.

There is more than one way in which the boardsailor can improve his technique. Depending on the requirements of the situation at the moment, the choice is between a quick tack and a shooting tack: the photo series on the following pages show the sequence of movements for both.

A **quick tack** is used when the aim is to alter course quickly using the minimum of space, for example to tack into a small gap in the front row at the start of a race, or to avoid a collision, or sometimes when approaching the finish. Because the radius of the turn is small the board comes almost to a halt, but it picks up speed again very quickly as soon as the tack is completed.

Phase I	Pull the sail right in, and rake the rig aft vigorously. Keep both feet aft of the mast and place one leg aft of the daggerboard to start the turn.
Phase II	Pull the sail back beyond the board's centreline. The effect of this is to accelerate the board and later to turn it quickly.
Phase III	Once the board is head-to-wind, catch hold of the mast underneath the boom with your mast hand, and move your front foot up to the mast.

◁ *Ex-World Champion Marie-Annick Maus, tacking using the mast hold technique*

Thrusting the stern down into the water accelerates the turn

Phase IV	As soon as the bow has turned through the wind, move to the other side of the board taking several small steps. As you pass forward of the sail, which is empty of wind, exchange hands so that your former sail hand holds the mast.
Phase V	As you turn your body on what is now the windward side of the board, quickly pull the rig forward with your mast hand, catch hold of the boom with your back hand and pull in the sail

The rig should be raked rather farther forward than its normal closehauled position, so that you make a sort of pumping action while sheeting in the sail; this will accelerate the board from an almost dead stop to its normal speed.

If the board has a smooth underwater surface aft and little volume near the stern, such as a Windsurfer or Mistral Competition, the turn can be speeded up by shifting your weight aft; this thrusts the stern under the water, causing it to sheer sideways.

Quick tack with the mast hold technique (above)
a. The sail is hardened in to initiate the tack
b. The rig is raked right back. One foot is at the base of the mast and the mast hand grasps the mast

c. Jump round the mast, which is passed to the new mast hand
d. The rig is pulled back up and to windward
e. The sail hand catches hold of the boom and pulls in

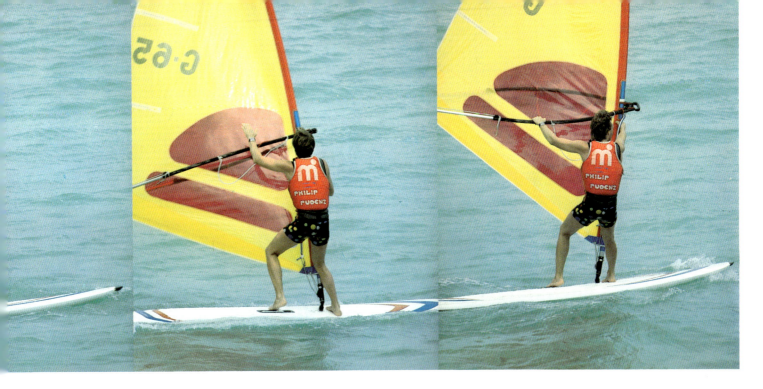

In contrast to the quick tack, *the object of the shooting tack (below) is to gain as much ground to windward as possible while going about. Every* stage should be taken gently and smoothly, so as to lose the minimum of way.

The **shooting tack** is slower and has a larger radius; it is used when the aim is to gain as much ground to windward as possible while losing the minimum of speed. (See previous pages, above.)

Phase I	Tilt the board slightly farther to leeward with your feet and rake the rig slowly aft; keep both feet close behind the mast.
Phase II	Avoid immersing the stern by keeping your weight as near the middle of the board as possible; keep it trimmed in the most favourable way. Rake the rig aft with your arms and pull it only slightly to windward of the centreline.
Phase III	When the board is head-to-wind, place one foot forward of the mast and prepare to go about by catching hold of the mast with your mast hand.
Phase IV	Keep the sail sheeted in, take two steps round the mast (more slowly than for a quick tack) and then rapidly harden in the sail on the other side.
Phase V	Again, rake the rig forward and slightly to leeward after tacking so that you can make one or two pumping movements to counter any possible loss in board speed which may have occurred.

It is important to avoid shaking the board or waving the rig about while tacking because these have a braking effect on speed through the water.

In both types of tack, the stage when the sail is empty of wind and slatting should be as brief as possible since at this point it produces no forward drive.

Gybing
a. The turn is initiated by shifting weight farther aft
b. The windward edge is weighted
c. The rig is raked aft and sheeted in
d. Change mast hands and
e. sail hands, and sheet in

Gybing

It is not only beginners who are anxious about gybing a sailboard. In a gybe the *stern* is turned through the wind so that the wind blows against the opposite side of the sail.

As with tacking, the first type of gybe that is learned could be called the **safety gybe**. Again, you turn the board with your feet while holding the sail, empty of wind and shaking, away from the side towards which the board is turning. Like the safe tack, this method of gybing is slow because the shaking sail produces no propulsion for a relatively long time.

It must be admitted, however, that a pure, quick racing gybe involves a certain risk even for the best windsurfers, and when watching a race it is clear that most people opt for a compromise between a fast gybe and a safe one. They are certainly wiser to take slightly more time gybing than to risk a fall, which could cost them many places if the worst came to the worst and involved touching a mark of the course.

c

A   B

D   E

17

The photographs (opposite) show the phases of a **fast gybe**:

Phase I   From a beam reach or broad reach, slowly rake the rig to windward. Keep both feet level with the daggerboard slot so as to avoid reducing speed by shifting weight too far aft.

Phase II   To accelerate the turn, shift your weight to the edge of the board which is outside as you turn. This is the moment at which you are least stable, so bend both knees and hips a little, to lower the centre of gravity of your body. In this slightly crouched stance you are ready to react quickly and can use your muscles to apply leverage.

Phase III Turn the stern through the wind before gybing the rig, but keep the sail in its original position until the turn is completed; rake the mast even farther aft and sheet in again to make the stern turn faster.

Phase IV   Now catch hold of the mast just underneath the boom. With one quick movement lean the rig to the new windward side, simultaneously releasing the boom with your sail hand, and pass the mast forward of your body to your new mast hand. This concludes the forward/windward movement of the rig.

Phase V   Now grab the boom with your back hand and sheet in the sail. Distribute

A   B

your weight on your feet so that the board sails level or slightly tilted.

This basic sequence can be varied as necessary. The farther aft you shift your weight at the start of the gybe, the smaller the radius of the turn will be, as is shown in several of the photos later in this book. In light airs, gybe the rig earlier so that you have enough time to incorporate a pumping movement as you sheet in. In heavier winds, however, keep the rig on the original gybe as long as possible; then, when your sail hand releases it, the boom will swing round instantly and you can grasp it immediately with your new sail hand. You can decrease the projected sail area by tilting the rig and this will reduce the pressure when you sheet in.

Practise both tacking and gybing in easy conditions when the wind is light and the water smooth. Once the sequence of actions has become automatic and you feel quite sure, you can try it in stronger winds and more disturbed water until the time comes when you are confident of your technique whatever the conditions.

When practising, it is best to find a small buoy or float so that you can check the radius of the turn and the time your manoeuvre takes.

Gybing in a strong wind
a. The board continues to plane
b. The body's centre of gravity stays low
c. Weight is placed carefully on the outside edge
*d. **The inside foot controls the new windward edge***

C   D

The Start

A good start depends on three factors: the psychological situation, tactics against your opponents and the technique that gives you real board control. It bears repeating that board control is so vital that without it you cannot hope to deal with the other factors.

In every case it is a question of 'How can I get into the position I have chosen and how can I stay there?' or 'How will my position alter before the starting signal is made?'

All the suggestions that follow can be practised with a float or buoy if there is no line available.

Surfmarathon at St Moritz

First, sail on starboard tack at about 45° to the wind, approach as close as possible to the buoy and then wait there, stopped, with your sail slatting. When you lie like this you will drift downwind at an angle of about 135° to the wind.

To avoid sagging to leeward of the imaginary starting line, sheet in the sail slightly with your sail hand and you will then move at 90° to the wind, exactly along the line. The speed at which you drift sideways will of course depend on the strength of the wind, and you will need to experiment to find out the rate at which the board drifts.

One method of reducing leeway is to sheet in the sail occasionally so that you can sail a couple of metres

Fighting for the best starting position on the line

closer to the line. The board will be almost head-to-wind when you have done so, and will have to be turned back to an angle of about 45° to the wind by your feet.

Manoeuvring in such restricted space makes great demands on a boardsailor's sense of balance, especially when there are waves.

In order to have as much room as possible to move the rig freely, it is best to stand fairly far forward on the board, with one foot ahead of the mast. Then, if the wind shifts suddenly and threatens to push you over

Shortly after the start of a World Championship race

into the water, you can escape by moving forward of the mast.

Experience also shows that you react quicker if your front hand grasps the mast below the boom, as shown in the photo.

If the board drifts so far from your chosen position that it is not possible to return to it as described above, you can take two tacks to sail back to it (provided your place has not been taken by any of your opponents). To do this you need to know how to tack on the spot. Sheet in the sail, pulling the clew slightly to windward

of the centreline. The board will not start to move ahead or backwards but it will be pushed slightly sideways. With your feet, now turn the board under the rig and tack quickly. Sail to your chosen position and pull the rig over to windward of the centreline so as to brake the board, and you can then tack on the spot again.

Should you have too little room to do this, or if you fear that a competitor will ask for water when you are on port tack without the right of way, an alternative method is to sail stern first. You will not find this easy initially because the fin will cause the board to sheer off quickly to one side, but you can prevent the stern from turning to windward if you rake the rig really far aft.

Philip (white sleeves) is standing still correctly. △

Charly goes about again onto starboard tack. ▷
Philip tries to stay in his chosen position by sailing backwards

Again, it is best to have one hand on the boom and one on the mast.

Once you are sailing forwards again, you can try to make ground to windward.

◁ *Safe stance while waiting on the line: one foot foreward of the mast and a hand holding it*

◁ *Just before the start; Charly (at the right) has drifted too far and tacks*

Closehauled Sailing

Some more skilful beginners let themselves get carried away by the exhilaration of beam-reaching at speed, but the challenge of working to windward does not only appeal to those who are interested in racing. The problem that faces every boat sailor or windsurfer is to find the right compromise between sailing fast and pointing close to the wind. Broadly speaking, beating is actually the easiest part of boardsailing.

It is only when one's performance when closehauled sailing is compared with that of others that the benefits of practising technique are revealed, and training in company is undoubtedly the best way to find the right compromise between board speed and pointing high.

Virtually all boards sail faster when closehauled if they are tilted slightly to leeward, the reasons being first that the lateral area is increased when you immerse the edge of the board by thrusting it down to leeward, and secondly that leeway is countered by the whole area of the daggerboard, which is exactly at right angles to the direction of pressure. The projected lateral area and thus its resistance to sideways movement is reduced when a board is tilted to windward.

It is well known that sailboards such as those in the Open Class (Division II) have a tendency to capsize in stronger winds. Should this happen when wind speed is unexpectedly low, there are several possible reasons. One is that the sailboard could be heading off the wind, with the result of not pointing high enough being excessive side force on the long centreboard. Alternatively, the clew of the sail could have been pulled too far to windward of the centreline, which also causes too much side force and leverage to leeward through your feet. A third possibility, when the wind is stronger, is that your feet are not as near to the edge of the board as they should be.

It is when the board is just on the point of capsizing that the right compromise between speed and pointing close to the wind is achieved. To keep the board trimmed in this optimum position, one foot is used to

Closehauled technique

Charly sailing a displacement board closehauled: it is tilted to leeward ▷

apply downward pressure on the top of the board while the other foot has to keep the board continuously at the correct angle.

If the wind increases so much that there is a real danger of capsizing when the sail is fully sheeted in, rake the centreboard 5° farther aft than its normal angle of about 15° (measured at the leading edge). Although the board will not point quite so well it will sail considerably faster.

It is at the intermediate stage, when you are changing from displacement sailing to a semi-planing condition, that it is especially worthwhile sacrificing pointing high in order to benefit from the considerable increase in speed.

As on other points of sailing, your weight should be positioned on the board in such a way as to reduce its resistance to the minimum. If you are too far forward

Hands close together; this is ex-World Champion Niko Stickl

the bow will tend to dip into the water, and if you are too far aft the stern will be immersed: severe drag is caused in either case. Keep your feet as close together as you can especially when conditions are difficult, for instance when there is a sea; taking weight off (unweighting) the bow and stern and concentrating it in the middle of the board reduces the up and down motion (pitching).

For maximum efficiency hold the rig upright. When closehauled the clew is normally pulled in as far as the centreline, but in smooth water you can even pull it slightly over to the windward side.

In order to avoid disturbing the airflow over the sail, keep your body as far from the rig as possible. The

Robby Naish on the beat. His feet are close together and controlling the board

problem in light airs is that the rig has to be held both upright and away from the body, and there are two alternatives – either to bend the elbows and wrists and hold the rig close to you, or to 'clamp' the boom with your back arm. It is up to the individual to decide which method he prefers. Those who advocate the first say they find they are more sensitive to the pressure of the wind on the sail, although it is not so easy to feel this when your wrists, and elbows are sharply bent. Those who prefer the latter method emphasize that the rig is upright, but their bodies are closer to the sail.

In both cases avoid shaking either the board or the rig. Every movement of the board, however small, causes turbulence in the water, while sudden move-

ments of the rig disturb the smoothness of the airflow over the sail.

Wind strength is not always matched by the height of the waves; they are generally smaller when the wind is offshore, but when the wind is easing or blowing onshore higher waves may persist. It is often preferable to sail slightly more free and go for speed when waves are short because they slow the board continuously. If seas are higher and longer, and the board sails up and down them, a gently undulating course is better. As you sail down the wave the board accelerates, and you have to bear away slightly because increase in speed makes the apparent wind come more from ahead; when climbing up the wave you can head up again because the apparent wind frees (comes more from the side) as board speed drops.

Reaching

Board designs differ, and technique when reaching across the wind therefore depends on whether you are sailing an all-round board of the Mistral Competition or Windglider or Windsurfer type, or one of the newer generation of Open Class boards. As a general rule, it can be said that mastering the basic handling of flat boards is relatively easy but that technique has to be adapted for rounder boards.

For both types optimum trim is maintained in lighter winds by avoiding putting too much weight on either the bow or the stern. The board should lie flat on the water and not be tilted to leeward. The daggerboard must be lowered fairly far in light breezes, because at slower speeds leeway would be excessive and the board too unstable with the daggerboard raised; furthermore, the hydrodynamic properties of most daggerboards are much worse when they are raked aft. When a daggerboard is withdrawn entirely, the additional drag caused by turbulence around the open slot is excessive.

Essentially, then, sail with the daggerboard down, keep the board flat and control your course by steering with your feet. Capsize falls generally result from

Reaching technique: feet and body positions are different from the closehauled stance

changing direction too suddenly: this causes a change in the flow of water streaming over the daggerboard, which then sheers upwards.

It has proved helpful to stand with your body turned to face slightly forwards while your back foot is roughly amidships, placed at right angles to the direction of sailing so that you can use your ankle to control the tilting angle of the board along its length. You push the board slightly to leeward with your foot. Your front leg is stretched forward (see photo) in order to counter the forward pull of the rig, and your front foot is at an angle in between 45° and pointing

Reaching in a strong wind: the body's centre of gravity is low, the rig upright

forward. In this position it is easy to keep the board correctly trimmed.

In stronger winds and when the board is sailing faster, the resistance of a fully lowered daggerboard is so great that it is preferable to accept the alternative of poorer water flow with a raised daggerboard or open slot.

In order to remove the daggerboard, let go of the boom with your sail hand. The centre of gravity of the rig must be right over the board so that you can support it with one hand while you are pulling out the daggerboard. It is better to keep the rig fractionally to windward because if it started to fall you could then grab it quickly and pull in, whereas if it was over slightly to leeward you would have to let it drop.

The great majority of fast Open Class sailboards now have daggerboards designed so that they are operated by foot and can be raised half way or fully. They can be moved through a wide range of positions with the protruding lever. When altering the position of the daggerboard, the sail generally has to be let out for an instant to east the pressure on the daggerboard case.

Open Class boards with daggerboards removed or retracted are only stable when under way, and it is therefore advisable to lower the daggerboard at least part way when board speed drops, and before tacking and gybing.

Reaching with the daggerboard removed

A modified foot adjusted daggerboard ▽

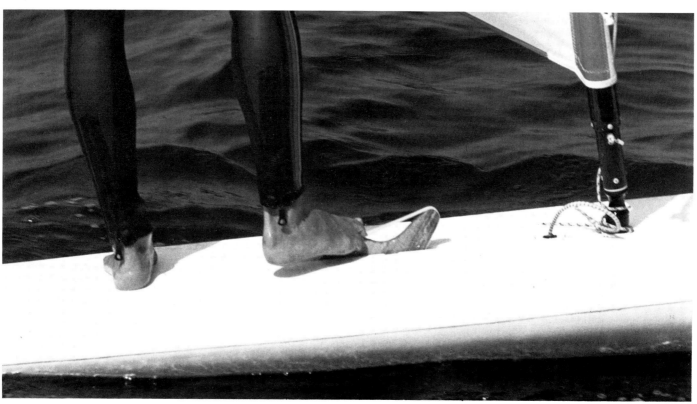

Downwind Sailing

Incorrect downwind technique: weight is too far aft and the rig is not held upright. Turbulence clearly visible at the stern causes drag

Beginners find that the most difficult stage is learning how to run downwind, and running makes even higher demands on performance as the wind blows harder. The main reason is the unstable state of the board and rig. Stability is relatively good when the wind acts laterally, i.e. when sailing close to the wind or reaching across it. Airflow is then laminar along the sail. Running downwind, however, with the sail at right angles to the wind air does not flow evenly over it and the pull of the rig is therefore much more difficult to

anticipate. Furthermore, because the direction of pull is forward, it does not contribute to lateral stability.

In light breezes difficulties of balance are still relatively slight, but again the windsurfer should try to move the board or rig as little as possible, in order to avoid reducing speed. It is also important not to immerse the stern by placing your weight too far aft. Keep your feet close together and your knees and arms bent, ready to react quickly. The rig should be upright so that you are using the whole area of the sail. When

33

the wind is stronger it is as well not to stand in a 'safe' position by moving your weight towards the stern of the board, because it is *not* safe. Even on a run it is better to sail with the daggerboard down for as long as you can, and you will find it is best to stand near or even slightly forward of it. In this position you can more easily avoid shifting weight from one side of the board to the other, which would cause it to sheer off sideways. The farther aft that you weight one side of the board, the more readily will it react by steering itself.

It is best to move your feet apart gradually as the forward pull of the sail increases at higher wind speeds. Shift one farther forward and one farther aft, in order to counterbalance the pull from the rig towards the bow and so that you can shift your weight onto the front or back foot at will. For example, when the bow dips into a wave you can put your weight momentarily onto the back foot, which should be pointing roughly across the board, and then shift it back to your front foot.

You can leave the daggerboard well down if the water is calm and the board is relatively steady in spite of a fairly strong wind, but if there are waves which you can sometimes surf down, the daggerboard should be half or fully raised. In strong winds, when the board will plane even on a run, there is a much greater danger of capsizing, and the daggerboard should be fully raised or removed.

The most secure stance is to bend your hips and knees more, so as to lower your centre of gravity. Although this is the best position because you react most quickly when you are crouching slightly, there are occasions when it is not suitable and other downwind positions should be used. In some extreme cases squatting or even sitting and lying back are preferable. When racing, the question of tactics comes into this, however, and will be considered later.

Good technique: feet correctly positioned just aft of the mast, rig upright. No turbulence from the stern

Two methods of running in a strong wind – crouching and sitting down

Everyone tries to stay clear of the others' windshadows

Rounding Marks

Pinching: the clew of the sail is hauled to windward of the centreline, and the board should be tilted farther than normal towards the lee edge

So far as technique is concerned, the rounding of marks is virtually the same as already described for tacking and gybing. Occasionally, however, particular techniques are needed for tactical reasons, and they differ from those used for normal manoeuvring.

If it looks as though you can almost fetch the first mark at the end of the starting beat, try to 'pinch', by pointing very close to the wind even though the result

will be a loss of speed. Pull the sail farther to windward of the centreline than usual, and tilt the board farther towards the lee edge to increase the effective lateral area and reduce leeway. If you fetch the mark you will have saved tacking twice unnecessarily, and at the

The lady sailing Windglider 833 neatly tricks her opponents by rounding the mark tightly

36

A

B

C

D

E

same time will have avoided the risk of losing even more ground should you have had to give way by bearing away when on port tack in a congested fleet.

You may find yourself in a situation where you have to be able to gybe on the spot, for instance when you are the outside board rounding the mark. Put your back foot so far aft that you can thrust the stern down into the water, and tilt the board slightly to windward. At the same time hold the rig right over to windward.

G65 (nearest the mark) is using the right tactic. He is clearly too far to leeward and is pinching so that he can make the mark without having to tack again. In this way he gains over his two immediate opponents

A

B

C

D

Should the board come to a complete standstill when gybing, push the sail well over to windward with your sail hand so as to force the board round even faster onto its new course. Dragging a foot in the water as a brake may facilitate the turn, but under the Racing Rules (Rule 60.1) this is not permitted in competition.

Gybing on the spot: the radius of the turn is small
a. *Extreme weighting of the stern*
b. *Heavy pressure on the side that is outside when turning*
c. *Mast hands exchanged*
d. *Mast raked to windward*
e. *Sheeting in*

E

A

B

720° Turns

In the Racing Rules, race committees may permit alternative penalties for minor breaches, usually concerning rights of way, so that disqualifications can be avoided. The Sailing Instructions for boardsailing races often state that the two full circles penalty, the 720° turn, is permitted. It must be carried out clear of the other boards, and the penalised board has no rights of way over the others while performing the 720° turns.

As when tacking and gybing, there are two ways of doing a 720° turn; the passive method is slow, but the active one is much faster. In the slower method you support the rig by the uphaul, letting go of the boom and allowing the sail to lose drive and slat freely while you turn the board round with your feet. The quicker method, with the sail sheeted in and driving, is obviously preferable. Although you should avoid breaking the rules, incidents are bound to occur fairly frequently when racing in close company and one has to remember that it is still possible to save the situation by performing a perfect 720°.

The 720° penalty turn has to be performed as follows:
'The turns may be made in either direction but both in the same direction, with the second full 360° turn following immediately on the first.'

A sailboard is much more manoeuvrable sailing backwards than a boat, mainly because the rig can be moved about so freely, and a 720° can be performed considerably faster backwards because the daggerboard digs down into the water and keeps the turning radius very small, while the bow, without a protruding fin, pivots round much faster than the stern would.

When turning the board with your feet, adopt a slightly bent stance in order to help balance by keeping your centre of gravity low, and rely more on the pulling of the rig.

720° turn (above and right). With the sail in, the board is turned 360° with the feet. The body's centre of gravity is kept as low as possible. The penalty consists of sailing two of these turns.

C

D

E

F

41

Trapeze Harness

This accessory not only increases the pleasure of sailing for the occasional boardsailor who is less than really fit, but is also permitted in various classes (e.g. Open Class, Mistral, Windsurfer and Funboards). It eases the strain on hands and arms, and helps those whose muscles have been trained for short high loading or movement (dynamic work), perhaps through involvement with other types of sport, rather than for endurance and holding on for extended periods (static work). With a harness you can sail longer and be fully in control when wind speeds are high. Without one, sailing in conditions such as those at the Pan Am World Cup at Hawaii would be unthinkable.

Do not depend entirely on a harness, however. It is inadvisable to use one when practising or racing in unsteady winds because it is the ability to recognize changes in wind direction as well as sudden increases in wind strength that is decisive. These should be registered through your hands so that you can react quickly and correctly. However, when the wind is stronger, and particularly when it is steady, you need to save all your concentration and strength for tactics, gybing, tacking and to keep the board sailing at maximum speed.

A harness with a long back support which reaches over the lumbar vertebrae has proved to be especially effective when sailing for longer periods. The length of the trapeze lines on the boom should be such that your arms are slightly bent when you are hanging on the boom. If your arms are fully stretched your muscles take longer to react, but if they are bent too much leverage is poor because you are too close to the rig, and your reactions will be adversely affected.

It is easiest to use a harness on the beat, when the pull on the sail is greatest but corrections to sail trim are relatively small. Generally speaking, when you are hooked onto the harness line you should try to swing in such a way that the boom only moves up and down and not towards you, because you will then disturb the airflow on the sail less.

Philip demonstrating optimum trapeze adjustment

Given a little practice, the harness can also be used when beam-reaching and broad-reaching in fairly fresh winds when the daggerboard has been raised or withdrawn. Here again, it is better to use the harness when the water is smooth rather than in waves.

It is impossible to use the trapeze on the run. Because the sail is stalled (i.e. not producing lift) there is comparatively little pull from the rig, even at higher wind speeds, but the main problems are caused by the technique necessary to control the board.

Trapeze set too short and too long, compared to proper adjustment which allows the arms to be slightly bent

COURSES, STARTS AND FLAG SIGNALS

Committee boat shortly before the starting gun. Its distinctively marked mast defines one end of the line

The classic course used for racing both boats and sailboards, particularly at championship level, is triangular. Because of its shape it provides upwind (beating) work, reaching and running legs. The most frequently used type of triangular course is the Olympic triangle.

The Olympic Course

This course has been clearly defined and is not only used for Olympic racing but also for most of the World, European and National championships for boards and dinghies. There are three windward legs, two broad-reaching legs and one downwind run, and the ends of the legs are marked by three buoys or marks laid in a triangle.

Olympic race organization is based on sailing the course anti-clockwise, but otherwise Sailing Instructions often leave it open as to whether the course will be sailed anti-clockwise (red board or flag), the marks being left to port, or clockwise (green board or flag), marks left to starboard.

The first leg begins after crossing a starting line which is laid somewhat downwind of mark 3 and at 90° to the wind direction; its length depends on the number of competitors and any natural limitations or hazards. The opening beat takes the boards upwind to mark 1, and is followed by two reaching legs, each at

Olympic course

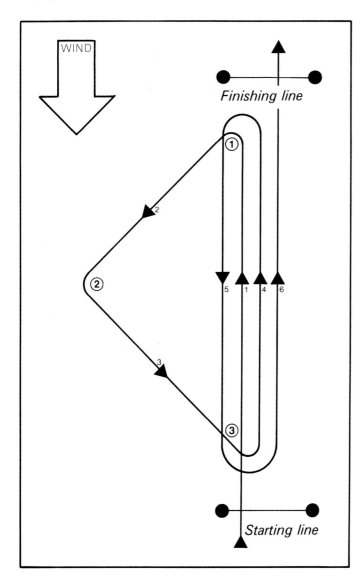

Triangular 'Kiel Week' course

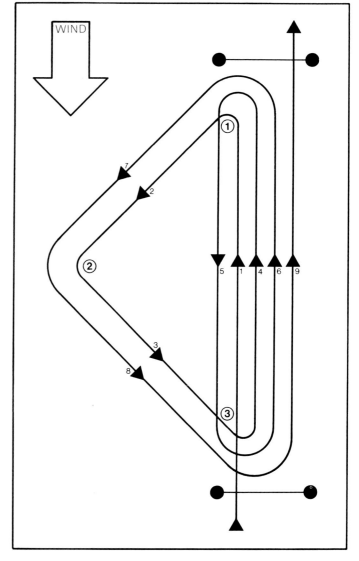

an angle of 135° to the wind. Mark 2 at the end of the first broad reach is rounded by gybing. After rounding mark 3 the 'sausage' follows; the boards beat up to mark 1 again and then run back. When mark 3 has been rounded the second time the boards beat back to cross the finishing line, which is laid slightly upwind of the triangle. It is also at 90° to the wind like the starting line, but generally shorter.

Triangular (Kiel Week) Course

An alternative triangular course (named after the hundred year old Kiel regatta) can be used where there is not enough water to provide legs as long as are stipulated for an Olympic course. The triangle and the 'sausage' of the Olympic course are followed by another triangle and often yet another sausage so as to provide a race of adequate length. The angles between the legs may also have to be set to suit the water available.

The ratio of windward work to reaching and running legs varies from approximately 3:3 to 4:5.

Timing and Flag Signals

A race does not begin when the Starting signal is made; this is preceded by Warning and Preparatory signals. (These are detailed more fully in IYRU Racing Rules, Part II.)

When windsurfers first started to race, these signals were made 6 minutes and 3 minutes before the starting signal for the warning and preparatory signals respectively. These are shorter intervals than is normal for sailing boats, and organizers have reverted to the 10 minute (Warning) and 5 minute (Preparatory) signals. Sound signals (guns) are made simultaneously with the visual signals, which are made with flags or boards. Timing is taken from the visual signals.

It is important to note that visual signals take precedence over sound signals since, for example, the signal gun could fail to fire or be late, or it could go unheard by some competitors resulting in an unfair advantage to others.

Scoring Systems

There are several points systems which can be used when a series of races is being run, and this is the most common form of racing. The Olympic points system is used frequently for other events. (IYRU Racing Rules, Appendix 5.)

The series consists of 7 races, the 6 best of which are counted; if 6 races are sailed, 5 count, if 5 races, 4. A minimum of 5 races is required for the series (this ruling generally applies only for championships). The winner of the series is the person with the lowest total of points accumulated from the various races.

Finishing place	Points
1st	0
2nd	3
3rd	5.7
4th	8
5th	10
6th	11.7
7th and following	Placing+6

Points are awarded to all participants who finish the race correctly. Those who retire or are disqualified are given points equal to the number of competitors entered for the series plus 1.

If a competitor is materially prejudiced, and fails to finish through no fault of his own, say by being hindered by one of the race officer's boats, the jury may give redress by adjusting his score. For example, they may award him points based on his position at the time of the incident, or on rounding the mark before the incident. Another alternative is to award points equal to the average of all the preceding races, or the average of all the races except the worst one and the one in question.

When the scores are level, the competitor who has obtained the most first, second, third places (etc) is placed higher. If there is still a tie, it stands as part of the final series results.

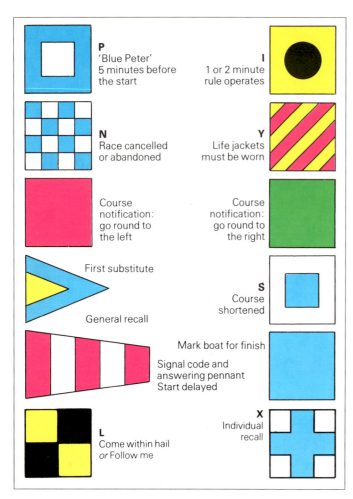

P		'Blue Peter' 5 minutes before the start
I		1 or 2 minute rule operates
N		Race cancelled or abandoned
Y		Life jackets must be worn
		Course notification: go round to the left
		Course notification: go round to the right
First substitute		General recall
S		Course shortened
Mark boat for finish Signal code and answering pennant Start delayed		
L		Come within hail *or* Follow me
X		Individual recall

Note: Other signals may well be used, especially for course or safety instructions. Always check Race Instructions.

A few seconds after the starting signal

The following abbreviations are used in results lists when the Olympic Points system is used:

DNC Did not compete	Did not rank as a starter under Rule 50.
DNS Did not start	Ranked as a starter under Rule 50 but failed to start the race.
PMS	Started prematurely or otherwise failed to comply with the starting procedure.
RET	Retired
DNF	Did not finish
DSQ	Disqualified
YMP	Yacht materially prejudiced

There are alternative points systems such as the RYA Long Series with points awarded as for the Olympic system, whereas the RYA Short Series points are based on points=place except for the winner who receives $\frac{3}{4}$ of a point. Then there is the German DSV points system, consisting of 6 races of which the best 5 count. The main difference from the Olympic system is that, instead of there being an advantage for the first 6 places, only the first 3 benefit: 1st=0 points, 2nd 1.6 points, 3rd 2.9 points, 4th (etc) points=place. If the object is to reward a certain percentage of the competitors, the Olympic points system is most suitable for board racing because there are usually over 30 starters.

To complete the picture it must be said that formerly a sailboard series often consisted of more than seven races, two or more of which could be discarded. Now, however, there is a clear tendency to stick ever more closely to sailing boat practice.

TACTICS

Camden P.L.

There are few sports in which tactics can be used in such a multiplicity of ways as racing boats and boards.

It is not enough to learn technique; success is almost impossible without basic tactical skill, and sailing tactics are fascinating because there are so many possibilities.

What is required is a combination of perception, a basic knowledge of tactics and the Racing Rules, and most important of all, the ability to make decisions quickly and act on them immediately. There are innumerable possible courses from the start to the finish line, but only the first person to finish can be said to have chosen more or less the best course.

It is a widely held misconception that tactics are purely a question of natural bent and talent. Some sailors learn more quickly of course, but anybody can

Resting or concentration – or both?

learn the groundwork of tactics. If success is going to be more than just a flash in the pan, tactical knowledge has to be added to one's technical skills.

There are three stages to each tactical decision. First, there is the awareness and analysis of the state of the race at that instant; these lead on to the second stage which is the process of establishing the theoretical situation. The last step is to execute the solution by putting theory into practice. The three stages are very closely linked and complementary; as with a mathematical calculation, an error in perception or analysis at the first stage means that the final result will be a failure.

It is impossible here to provide a tactical solution to every imaginable situation because the possibilities that could arise are endless. The following sections attempt to give the 'building blocks' with the aid of which a solution can be found to most of the problems that arise in the course of a race.

Psychological Attitude

The successful use of tactics cannot be considered separately from perfect technique, but equally important is the ability to analyse the situation and to adjust psychologically to the competition. To some extent it is these factors that are the driving force behind technique and tactics.

The first problem to decide is which race to enter, and initially you have to decide what is your level of performance. The first step on the road to success is certainly not to enter for a major race with a large number of competitors before you have competed in smaller local races at your own club. Even though you may not expect major triumph immediately, it is better to be able to see a little daylight at the end of the tunnel, in other words to avoid utter failure. Every boardsailor who is starting to race is therefore advised to take part in club races and training events, or in races with only a small number of competitors where pressure is not so great, and analysing what happened later is not so complicated. As you gain confidence you can enter more important events, but on no account should you plunge hesitantly into a race because psychologically you would lack confidence in your own ability. You need to be able to assess your skill correctly if you are to succeed. Everyone learning to race should bear in mind the fact that the target which you set yourself, whether you achieve it or not, is more important than the actual result. Of course your personal goal should be upgraded over the course of time to match your improved performance, but you should never lose the sense of what is attainable. For example, in your first race the aim can be to finish the course; then, not to be last; and later on, to finish in the first third of the field. These goals should be decided by each individual for himself before a race.

No race is like another. During each one a board-sailor has endless opportunities to improve his position or to drop back, and here again the right psychological attitude helps to overcome a situation. As is the case in other sports, the limit of a person's physical performance is generally considerably beyond his psychological preparedness to perform to that limit. When two good sailors set off on the first beat, one can be so determined that he corrects his mistakes and concentrates better, whereas the other may worry over past mistakes, lose confidence and motivation, and give up.

It has been found from experience that, even in the case of top racers, winning a championship or getting a good place in a race depends very much on their psychological attitude to such a situation. It is an utter waste of time to sail on feeling disheartened, because there are opportunities to improve your position right up to the finish of a race. Everyone should therefore ask themselves before the start:

How well did I do in the last race? What placing should be my goal? Who are my main opponents? Which mistakes did I make last time, and how shall I avoid making them this time?

Dirty Wind and Blanketing

Before considering tactics from the start to the finish of a race, it is essential to know how the strength and direction of the wind are affected by a sail. This is a

G65 in the safe leeward position

Running: each board tries to avoid being blanketed

subject that beginners often fail to take into account.

The rig of every sailing craft causes airflow to become turbulent, and the result is that wind force (speed) is considerably affected; the direction of the wind on the lee side of the sail is also disturbed. The diagrams following show the area which has to be avoided, but equally this zone of dirty or disturbed wind can be used deliberately to slow down an

opponent. Its extent is governed by the strength of the wind; in a light breeze the affected zone extends over a considerably greater area than in a strong wind, and the zone moves farther aft as the wind increases (darker shaded area).

It is easier to work clear of the dirty wind zone when boards are closehauled because the area is then relatively small. There are far fewer opportunities to free your wind (get into clear wind) when you are reaching or running.

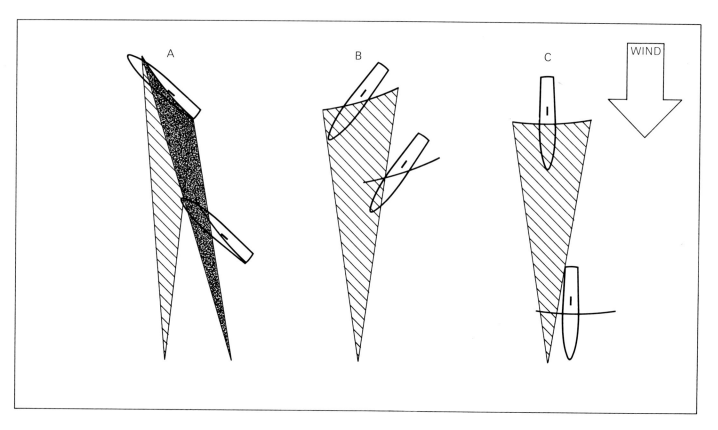

Typical wind shadows: closehauled, reaching and on a dead run

It is not only a case of the wind conditions being changed downwind of the sail, however, because in addition the actual direction of the wind is altered to some extent by the manner in which the sail converts the flow of air into forward propulsion.

The classic example of this is what is known as the safe leeward position (diagram). The wind, deflected from sail A, backwinds and disturbs B's sail and B consequently slows down to drop right back into A's dirty wind, where C has already been caught. C is hampered by the fact that the wind has been deflected by A's sail and is heading him; C therefore cannot point so high.

Your hands on the boom will generally register the fact that you have entered an area where wind is disturbed, and you should then free your wind quickly, either by altering course or by tacking away from the dirty wind zone.

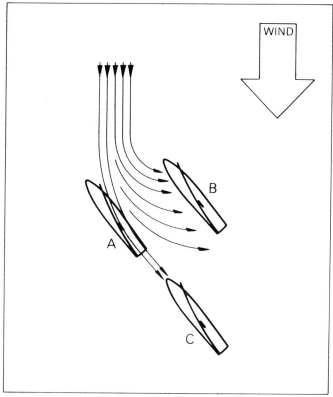

A is in the safe leeward position in relation to B

The fleet shortly before the start

The Start

It is in the preparatory period, even before the race has started, that people make the worst mistakes. When the customary method of starting is used, a good start is vital if you are to finish in the forefront of the race, while a mistake at this stage can make success unlikely, if not impossible, even before the starting signal has been made.

People often forget that a race does not start with the starting signal; no sooner has the preparatory signal been made than the boards begin to work themselves into some sort of order. This is not immediately obvious, as when marks are rounded by a succession of boards, but it happens nevertheless. Although one competitor may be only two metres astern of another at the starting line, his position may be such that he will be 200 metres astern of the same person only five minutes after the gun. This would certainly be an exceptional case, but it is far from impossible.

The necessity for a good start is even more vital when racing sailboards rather than boats, first because

of the high number of competitors – often over 100 gathered on the starting line – and second because the courses are shorter than sailing boat courses. A boardsailor has a shorter distance to sail to the first mark, which gives him less time and opportunity to get a clear wind in order to recover from a bad start.

The planning of a good start therefore involves factors which affect the race as a whole. The best start is not made by the person who crosses the line at the moment that the starting gun goes, but by the person who is in the most promising position some minutes later. The following points must be considered when planning where to start:

1. Which end of the line is favoured?
2. Will it be better to sail up the port side or the starboard side of the initial beat after starting?
3. Where is the first mark?
4. What is the opposition doing?

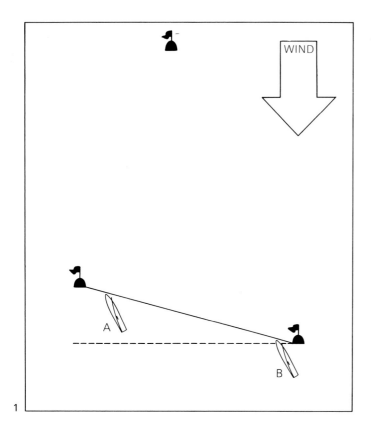

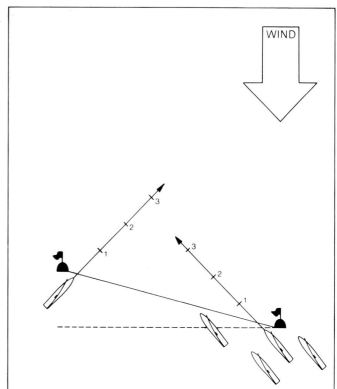

A has a shorter distance to sail to the first mark than B

A port tack start can be recommended here

The reason why you need to know which end of the line is better is because it is a shorter distance to sail from that end to the first mark than from the other end (Fig. 1).

There are several ways by which you can establish which is the preferable end:

a. When you are roughly in the middle of the starting line, bring the board head-to-wind. Stand forward of the rig and, holding the uphaul just below the boom, turn the board with your feet until the end of the boom is exactly over the centreline. The bow will now be pointing towards the better end of the line.

b. Sail exactly along the line in both directions. The tack on which you point closer to the wind takes you towards the preferable end.

c. At one end of the starting line (if possible the end marked by a limit buoy), shoot into the wind and extend one arm at right angles to the wind direction. Look along that arm to see whether the other limit mark is to windward or to leeward of the direction to which your arm points; if it is to windward you are looking at the preferable end.

The method you will use will vary according to the circumstances, such as how many competitors are crowded on the line, how big the waves are, local peculiarities of current or wind bends, and so on.

Coming to a decision as to which end is better is no cause for rejoicing, since at least half of the other competitors will have come to the same conclusion!

Which is the preferred end of the line?

Boards generally start with right of way, on starboard tack. To attempt to start on port tack is advisable only in exceptional circumstances, such as when there is a small fleet and a long starting line, but you must be sure before the final gun goes that there will be room for a port tack start (Fig. 2). Avoid the area at the better end of the line if it is very congested, because it would be very likely that you would have to give way to boards with right of way and would lose a lot of ground (Fig. 3). At worst, you could collide with another board and be forced to do a 720° penalty turn, losing vital minutes (and having to get clear of the others first) during which your chance of being among the leaders would disappear.

The best place to start when the port end is preferable is shown in Fig. 4, where A has the shortest distance to sail to the first mark and will not be hampered by the other competitors. It is rarely easy to get into this position, however, and you must be able to estimate very accurately the rate at which you will drift sideways during the last few minutes before the start. Frequently a dense crowd builds up just by the limit

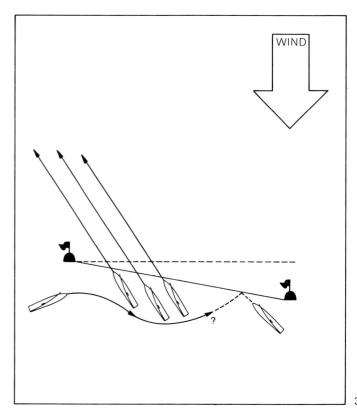

3

This time a port tack start is not promising

Karl Messmer, Z1, starts a funboard race successfully from a leeward position. He draws ahead of the fleet with a completely clear wind

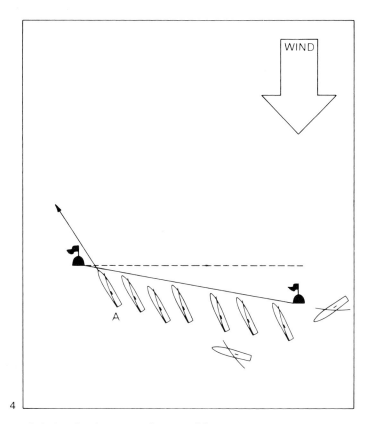

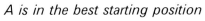

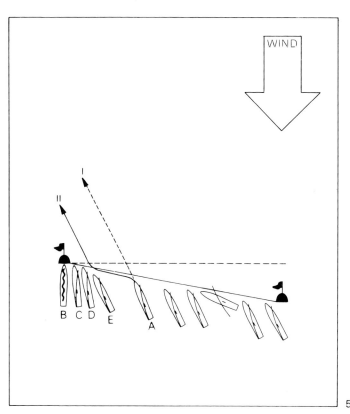

A is in the best starting position

A has two ways of making a good start
B will not make the mark
C, D and E are mutually hampering each other

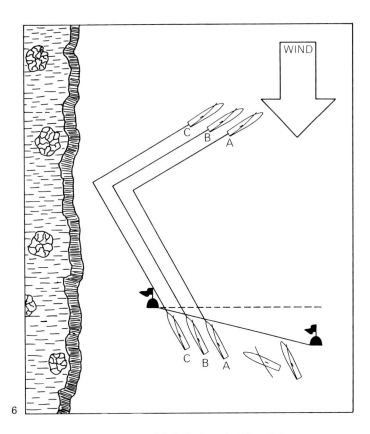
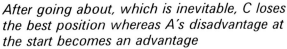

6

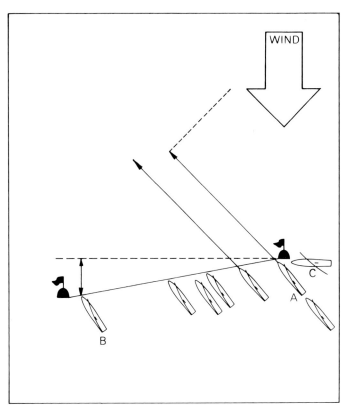

7

After going about, which is inevitable, C loses the best position whereas A's disadvantage at the start becomes an advantage

A has the best starting position. Right from the start, B is farther downwind than the rest. C is running a risk

mark, with the board farthest to leeward still trying to get past the mark on the correct side. A clear start could be ruined by touching the mark or another board, and the leeward board might not even lay the mark.

It is therefore advisable to decide first which end of the line is favoured, and then to keep clear of the crowd so that you have room to start at full speed (Fig. 5). Board A can then either leave some water to leeward (I) to avoid being hampered if board E sails into the safe leeward position, or can bear away (II) so as to accelerate during the last few seconds and sail past the massed boards immediately after the start (Fig. 5).

There is a further tactical advantage to starting in this way. If C or D cross the line too soon, there is every chance that they will be spotted and identified. A, on the other hand, will at least be hidden from the race officials at the port end by the other boards, and could even deliberately take the risk of starting too soon if he is so far from the other end of the line that he is unlikely to be identified.

Tactical considerations, such as the timing of the start or the path to be sailed after crossing the line, can also be the reason why what appears to be the 'best' starting position should be abandoned. For example, when the starting line is laid close to an obstruction or to the shore an advantage at the start can rapidly be transformed into a disadvantage (Fig. 6).

Strategy is also governed by circumstances when it is the starboard end of the line that is more favourable. The most advantageous position is to be the one who is farthest to windward, immediately by the mark or committee boat (Fig. 7) because it is from here that the distance to the first mark is shortest. Your timing must be very accurate if you are to manage to hold this position during the last minutes before the start, or to sail into this spot just when the race is being started. Here the only danger to A comes from competitors lying directly to leeward of him, who could get into the safe leeward position, but A would then still be free to tack away from them (broken line).

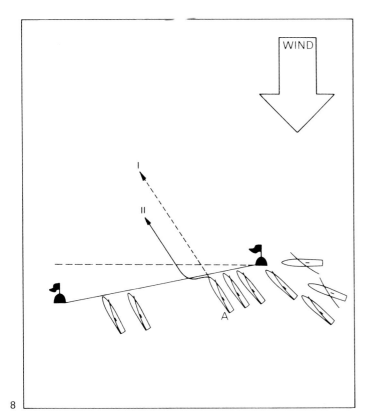

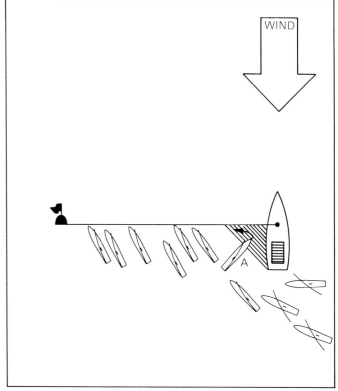

*A tries to start with clear wind, to leeward of
the crowd*

*A tries to stay in the dead corner by making
short tacks*

It is a known fact that congestion is particularly severe when it is the starboard end of the line that is favoured, because many racing sailors prefer to start at the committee vessel side. The result is crowding and in consequence boards may hamper each other. If you can be sure that your board speed is high enough, you can again try starting directly to leeward of such a windward group (Fig. 8). But good timing is absolutely essential if you try to do this because, should you drop back into the second row, you will have virtually no opportunity to clear your wind by going about onto port tack, also the tack on which you have to give way to all starboard-tack boards. Again it is just possible that you might dare to cross the line early in the hope of not being identified.

If you are unwilling to take this risk you can try to start in the second row, but you must then be right beside the mark so that you are free to get your wind clear by tacking onto port tack. As the committee vessel is often the limit mark of the starting line, there is generally an opportunity to manoeuvre into a dead corner to wait for the start. Skilful board handling in a very confined space is a prerequisite for this too.

Of course it often happens that the race officers lay the starting line exactly at 90° to the wind direction, and neither end is then preferable. This makes it difficult to decide which is the 'better' end and there are many possible places from which you can start with some hope of success. Again, and for the same reasons, it is best to start right at one end of the line. First, because when starting to leeward of the fleet at the port end, you could fail to lay the limit mark; second, you are more likely to be successful if you start near the starboard end in the safe leeward position some way to leeward of the boards massed by the limit mark; third, there is more chance of your being identified and recalled if you are over the line.

When the fleet is very large and the boards are massed all along the starting line, it is better not to start in the middle, both because the wind is less strong near

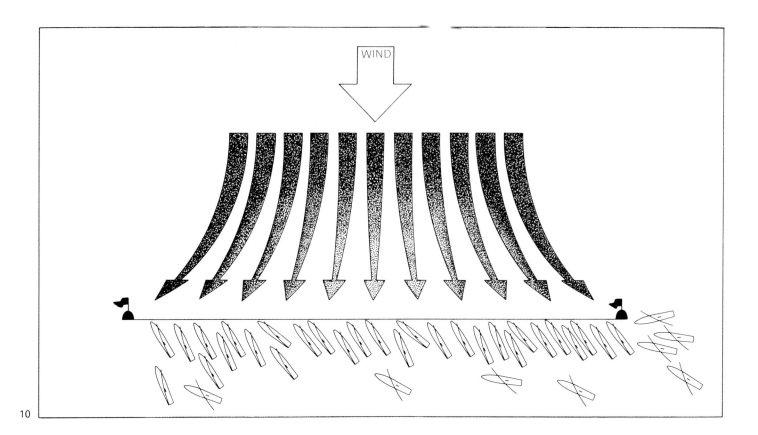

10

the centre on account of the resistance offered by the fleet as a whole, and because the wind id deflected by this 'obstruction' towards either side (Fig. 10). The consequence is that the boards on the port end of the line are able to point higher after the start, while those on the starboard side have to go about on port tack after the start before they can benefit from the wind bend.

the centre on account of the resistance offered by the fleet as a whole, and because the wind id deflected by this 'obstruction' towards either side (Fig. 10). The consequence is that the boards on the port end of the line are able to point higher after the start, while those on the starboard side have to go about on port tack after the start before they can benefit from the wind bend.

In spite of all this preparatory thinking about starting tactics, all your plans may be upset. For example, shortly before the start of a light weather race you might see a darkening on the water showing that there will be a breeze on the side which you consider to be the less favourable, and if you are sure that it is an indication that the wind there will freshen, you must then quickly abandon the idea of concentrating on getting the best starting position and instead sail over as fast as you can to this new wind, particularly if you think you can see (from a mark or from another sailing craft) that there is also a shift in wind direction from which you will be able to benefit (Fig. 11).

Some local peculiarities could be another reason why one side of the line is preferable to the other. For example, if you know that your best chance lies in

The wind is slowed and deflected as it approaches the mass of sails on the starting line. Towards the ends, however, it is strong right up to the line

making one long port tack close to the shore, you would probably be well advised to make full use of this fact and abandon any short-term advantage that starting at the starboard end might bring (Fig. 12).

The following general points should always be borne in mind by a boardsailor. When it comes to starting after a general recall, you should not let yourself be seen close to the line at a crucial time just before the start; you will then avoid being noticed by the race officers and recorders on the committee boat

A abandons his good starting position so as to be the first to reach the gust with its wind shift

A chooses the worse end of the starting line so as to be on the correct side of the course after the start

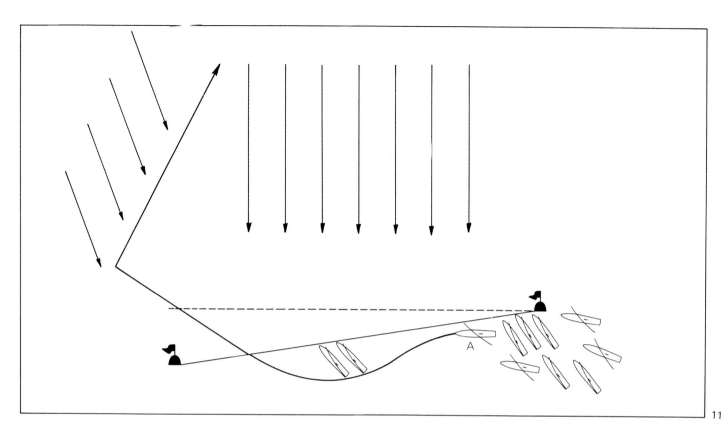

11

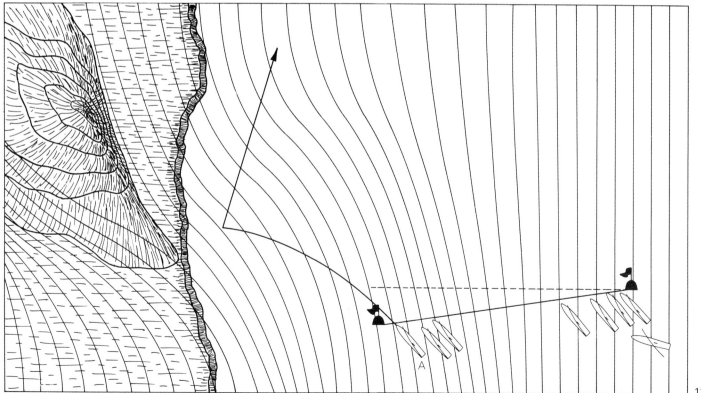

12

65

and elsewhere. They have a limited time in which to identify and note down anybody who is over the line at the start and, being human, they are more likely to recognize you and make a note of your number if you have been sailing in the vicinity for some time. At the start your trump card is to be inconspicuous, and that applies to the colour of your sail too – assuming that you have any choice in this matter. One board with a pretty multi-coloured sail, starting in a fleet of seventy with white sails is asking to be recalled at the start, as the photos show, and the race officers do not even need to read its number. Nor should the board itself be marked in any way conspicuously on the forward end, say by having a different coloured bow.

If you are bang on the line as the last few seconds tick by, it is advisable to hold your numbered rig as far aft as possible without losing your ability to manoeuvre, as shown in the photo.

It is absolutely essential to be able to manoeuvre freely during the period before starting. In so far as you can, avoid tricky situations and crowded water in which mass collisions may occur. One way to keep a little extra space for yourself on the line is to keep your board lying lengthwise along the line for as long as possible; then, when you turn the board onto a closehauled heading you will have a small space in which you can bear away and gather speed by trimming the sail.

Philip Pudenz at the World Championships in Israel. The rig is raked aft hiding the number so that the board will be less readily recognized in the event of making a premature start

The First Beat

Just as a good start can be said, in most races, to be the foundation on which a high place at the finish is built, completing the first beat among the leaders could be described as laying the first course of bricks. Tactics are of particular importance on the initial beat, because the vital decisions that determine one's placing at the finish have almost always been made by the time the weather mark has been rounded.

The most common mistake is failure to plan in advance. Many boardsailors leave it until after the starting signal before considering which side of the course is better, or what tactics to use in view of the weather conditions, their opponents or other external factors. The result is that they are unable to concentrate sufficiently on achieving maximum board speed, or that they fail to evaluate a change in the situation. The correct principle is to make use of the preparatory period before the start to gather all the information needed to solve the tactical problems that will arise, and to make an overall plan for the race.

The farther you sail into the shaded areas, the greater the chance of being caught out if the wind shifts

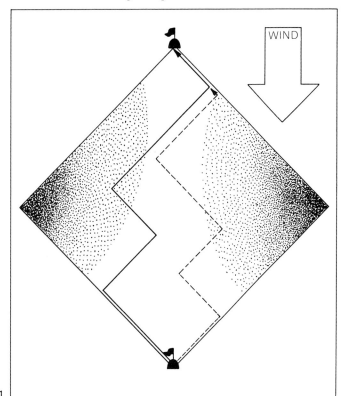

1

The information on which decisions are based includes the weather conditions, a thorough knowledge of the waters (e.g. the trend of the shore or the effect of a river current on the tidal stream), and any local peculiarities or topography that may affect the wind during the race.

The first essential is to establish the position of the first mark, because many of the decisions that will be made depend on this. For instance, knowing its position you can then estimate how far you can sail to one side of the course. Then there is the need to observe wind conditions where the race is being sailed. If you watch flags, other boardsailors or sailing boats you may be able to spot wind shifts from afar. When there are several races for a number of classes or weight groups and you are not in the first group, watch the preceding racers particularly closely while they are sailing the first beat, as far as time allows. Pay special attention to those who are taking a flyer and sailing right out to either side, because you can then usually decide whether one side of the course is preferable to the other.

In many waters the pattern of the waves differs at various parts of the course, and one should find out before the race where the waves will affect board speed; perhaps wave heights are considerably smaller over on one side of the course, or there is a rough patch to be avoided. Given all this advance information, you can start to build up a basic strategy. Should the situation alter at the start, however, you must be ready to adapt your strategy as necessary so that you can benefit from anything you have just observed, such as a wind shift.

In theory you can reach the first mark in two tacks, but even if the wind is completely constant in both direction and strength it is hard to decide when the right moment to tack has come. It is possible that the situation could be such that you have to concentrate on board speed alone, say in a very strong wind, but it is advisable to plan to make a short tack just before reaching the mark so that there is no risk of your overstanding it. Furthermore, even in the steadiest of winds minor wind shifts do occur and full use should be made of them.

There is normally no point in sailing on one tack beyond the point where you could lay the mark on the other tack, given the most favourable wind shift imaginable. The safe area is shown in the diagram.

There are two different types of wind shift; one type shifts continually in one direction, whereas the other behaves like a pendulum.

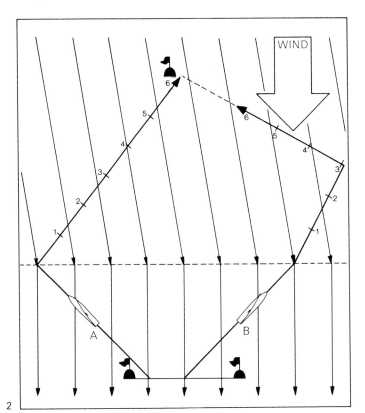

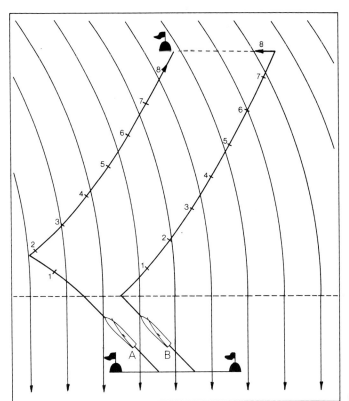

2

B is on the wrong side of the course when the wind shifts and heads him, and has a longer way to sail to the mark

3

A wins after an initial disadvantage, as he has held on towards the direction from which the new wind is to come and can then lay the mark

You can be forewarned about the former type. The force 4 westerly blowing at the time of the weather report on the morning of the race may be forecast to shift gradually to southwest, and assuming that the wind is still westerly at the start of the race, it will then be best to avoid sailing too far to the right-hand side of the course. Fig. 2 shows the way in which you would be affected if the wind shifted when you were halfway up the beat. If the shift is likely to be gradual, do not make the mistake of reacting by going about the moment that the wind starts to shift. As is clear from Fig. 3, although initially you may be at a slight disadvantage as a result of staying for a short time on what has become the worse tack, you will eventually reap a greater benefit from delaying your tack.

The other type of wind shift, the reversible or 'pendulum' variety, calls for tactics based on quick reactions. Every shift of wind that forces you to bear away should be used to your advantage by tacking quickly. In Fig. 4 you can see how A makes good use of every shift of wind as it occurs, while B reacts wrongly to the changes in direction.

If wind shifts occur in such quick succession that the loss of board speed due to going about cancels out the benefit gained by sailing on the correct tack, you should react only to the more important headers.

The ability to recognize a wind shift comes with experience, and the required observation can be practised both when training and during races. The method when on the beat is to check how the boards are pointing by sighting at a training partner or another competitor along the mast or through the window in the sail: when you meet next time (having tacked the same number of times) you can note the distance between you. If you take a bearing on the other competitors in this way after the start, you can get some idea as to which boards are as far to windward of the starting line as you are yourself.

At the start of a series, it is unwise to pick out one or more particular opponents to battle against. Quite apart from any other factors, you are only likely to succeed if other competitors are prepared to cooperate with you, and it is therefore better not to set off at the start of a race to blanket other boards and take their

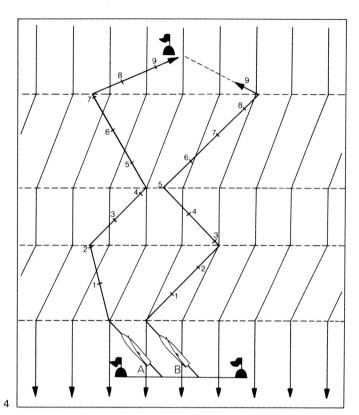

4

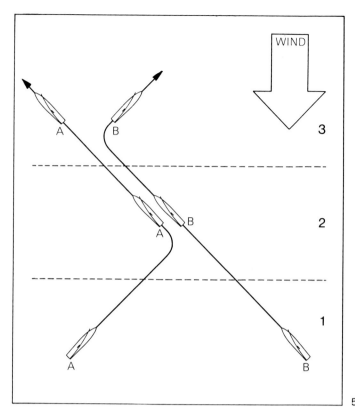

WIND

3

2

1

5

A has exploited each windshift to work up the line from his position at the time towards the mark, whereas B has made several wrong decisions

A tacks into the safe leeward position B is forced into going about

wind, but to concentrate instead on using correct tactics. Most important of all is to keep your own wind clear. Should you be unable to sail yourself into the leading row of boards after the start, the aim must be to sail as quickly as possible into a position where your wind is undisturbed and you can concentrate fully on achieving maximum board speed. It is particularly important to plan your actions in advance at the beginning of a race, rather than just considering what your nearest opponents are doing. If you do not do so, there is always the danger that you may miss out when there is a major change in the race situation, such as a wind shift, or you could lose track of the position of the first mark.

One bad mistake, made particularly by people who are just learning to race, is unfortunately seen all too often. They tend to be very aware of the recently learned right of way rules, and you can frequently see the pleasure on their faces when they meet another boardsailor approaching on port tack and are able to put him about. It is their right to do so, of course, and it can be advantageous in certain cases such as when

one wishes to tack just before reaching the weather mark, but in many situations what appears at first sight to be an advantage can often quickly become the opposite. If the other board succeeds in tacking close to leeward of you when you have right of way, any sudden loss of speed on your part may allow him to get into the safe leeward position, and there is then nothing that you can do except tack away from him (Fig. 5).

This puts you at a disadvantage in two ways: first, because you always lose speed when you go about; second, you should be sailing on starboard tack with a specific strategy in mind and good reasons for preferring one particular side of the course. If your opponent forces you into tacking, he will consider that he has outwitted you because he has managed to make you alter your strategy.

In spite of having right of way, an experienced boardsailor will often be seen to give away a small amount of ground by bearing away slightly in order to ensure that he is not forced to change his plans. Fig. 6 (page 76) shows how A, who bears away under B's

Funboards on the beat

stern shortly after the start, avoids being forced into changing his stretagy of sailing up the left-hand side of the course. It is clear, too, that if he had insisted on having right of way the result would be that he would have been caught in the dirty wind of boards C and D.

If, during the first part of the initial beat to the mark, you manage to sail into a position where you have got a clear wind, it is important to keep it clear all the way to the turning mark, and to improve your position if possible, because your placing at the finish depends to a large extent on the place in which you round the first mark.

It is the second half of the initial beat, together with rounding the first mark, that are really decisive. Halfway up the first beat there is room enough for many boards to sail in clear wind, but from that time on the pattern is usually one of a number of boards, all virtually level-pegging, forming themselves into a line close astern of one another. It is therefore a question of trying to avoid getting caught in another board's dirty wind, at the same time as avoiding losing ground to windward. It becomes increasingly difficult, however, to find a space as you get nearer to the mark.

Theoretically, you should look for clear wind close to the direct line to the mark, and only move to one side of the course at a later stage when you intend to tack for the mark. If you sail out too soon to a position from which you can lay the mark, it may happen that you are affected by competitors close by, and are slowed down in consequence; if the worst comes to the worst, you could even have to make another tack in spite of the fact that you could otherwise have fetched the mark.

When the course is sailed anti-clockwise, as is usual, you must be careful not to go for the mark from the left side of the course, since that means having to give way to all the boards that are approaching it on starboard

A

tack. If you stayed on port tack, you might well reach the mark in third place but be only the tenth board to round it because of having to wait for a gap into which you could tack (Fig. 7).

G65 is too late getting over to the side of the course where he would have right of way

C

B

a. Although he is ahead, he has to give way
b. . . . and loses valuable distance
c. Now he has to give way to another board
d. And, finally, he is last to round it and the loser

Following page:
In these breakers off the west side of Sylt,
facing the North Sea, tactical considerations
have a less important role

D

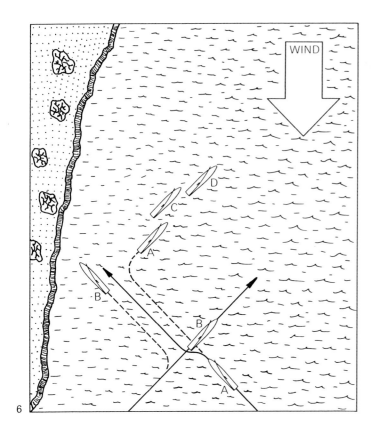

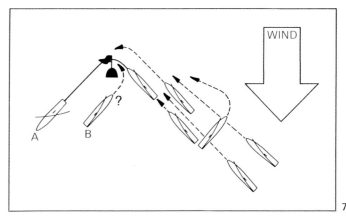

7

Although B is ahead of them, he will lose several places to the group that is approaching on starboard tack △
◁

A, preferring to sail to the better side of the course, does not enforce his right of way. He would otherwise have been forced to tack in order to clear his wind, and would then have been caught in the dirty wind of other boards
◁

The Reaching Legs

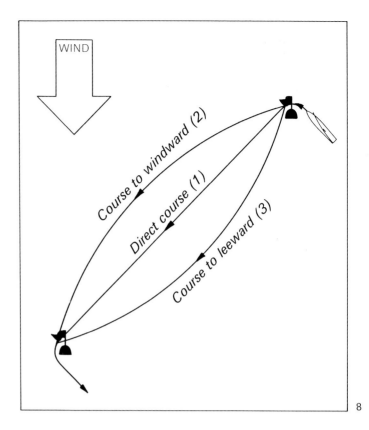

During the beat there are many opportunities to use tactics, and the tactics themselves have a decisive effect on what placing is achieved. On the reaching legs, however, tactical opportunities are much more limited, the main difference being that the line sailed between the two marks of the course is relatively straight. Nevertheless there are ways in which it is possible to reap a benefit when sailing the reaches. First of all, it is important to know the exact positions of the reaching and lee marks, because it is on these that you will base your tactics. Do not wait until you have rounded the weather mark before you establish the whereabouts of the reaching mark; you should know just where it is before finishing the first beat so that you can put the strategy you have planned into effect as soon as you start the reach.

The simplest situation is when the wind is steady and you cannot be blanketed by boards following astern. It is then a case of sailing the most direct line to the next mark, concentrating fully on board speed (Fig. 8). Such a situation is relatively rare, however, and variable winds and/or other boardsailors close by will generally cause you to deviate from the direct course. You then have two tactical alternatives, either to sail a curve to windward of the direct line, or one to leeward. Most board racers find from experience that the curve to windward is preferable since they can then keep clear of their opponents' dirty wind, but if there are many boards bunched close together you may find yourself being forced to luff farther to windward than you wish. The boards that are astern try to get to windward of those ahead of them, partly in order to avoid being blanketed by those still further astern and partly to blanket those ahead. The consequence is that the boards keep on luffing up, hindering and slowing each other as they do so.

If the angle of the course to the reaching mark is considerably less than 135°, it is advisable to choose the windward course. In such a case, even assuming that your board speed is greater it is not easy to break

World Championships in Florida. It can be seen clearly that, being so close to the mark, the sailor on port tack is finding it difficult to give room to the other competitors

through to leeward by sailing through an opponent's blanketing zone. Furthermore, if you are not too confident of sailing faster you can keep the boards astern of you in their places by luffing slightly to windward of the direct course, since they will not be able to break through your own dirty wind zone.

Any tendency of the wind to shift in direction will also affect your decision. In a wind that is light to moderate, most boards sail faster when they are pointing slightly higher than a broad reach, and you should therefore choose the windward curve if you expect the wind to head you.

In many other circumstances, however, it pays to choose the leeward curve, especially if you are in the middle of the fleet, because most of those to windward will disturb each other, and a lone board to leeward has a good chance of making up many places. Also, the leeward board has the advantage over the others when they meet at the reaching mark because it has right of way as the inside board, assuming of course that an overlap has been established before reaching the distance of two boards' lengths from the mark (Fig. 9). (See IYRU Racing Rules, Part IV, Section C.)

When one has the inside position with right of way he can decide how tightly to gybe round the mark, and

A

B

C

D

E

The same starting position: G65 defends his lead with a successful gybe close to the mark, and even increases it because the board following is not close to the mark

he should use this freedom of choice to gybe when he is still to windward of the mark so that he can luff up after rounding it. Experience has shown that board-sailors astern of you will often try to gain an advantage at the mark by shooting up to windward at full speed immediately after rounding it, with a view to blanketing those ahead.

A tactic that is often successful, perhaps after having dropped back several places on the first beat, is to sail to leeward of the direct course during the first reach so

A

B

C

D

Rounding the reaching mark. G65 sails too wide, and the boards astern can therefore sail into the gap between him and the mark. They then blanket him, and he loses two places while the other two each gain a place.

that, in the main, you are clear of your opponents' dirty wind, and will also be the inside board at the mark; you can then defend this position which you have earned by sailing to windward of the direct course during the second reach, and you will have the inside position again at the lee mark.

Although you will decide broadly which of these three alternative courses you will choose, the reach will not actually be straight because you still need to use

E

tactics and technique in order to benefit from waves and fluctuations of wind strength.

In moderate winds, if the waves are of normal size for the wind strength, your aim should be to accelerate by luffing up briefly so that, with the help of pumping, you reach the speed at which you can surf on the face of a wave. (Rule 60 of the IYRU Racing Rules defines the allowable means of propulsion, and 60.3 permits three rapidly-repeated trims and releases of the sail if done for the purpose of surfing, or getting onto the plane when planing conditions exist.) It often pays to abandon the direct course to the mark in order to keep on surfing longer, carried along as you sail down the steep face of the wave. Once that wave has passed beneath you, keep an eye open for the next promising wave and the opportunity to surf again. Thanks to the considerable speed at which you can surf like this, it is often possible to break through to leeward of another board, or to rush past one to windward by suddenly luffing up and blanketing him.

When the wind is so strong that you know you can plane, you will be able to start planing sooner if you luff up in the gusts, and bear away again once you are up on the plane. In most conditions you need to use both tactics and technique if you are to make the most of the combined effects of gusting winds and waves.

Observing the surface of the water carefully will give you an indication as to the strength of the wind. Darker

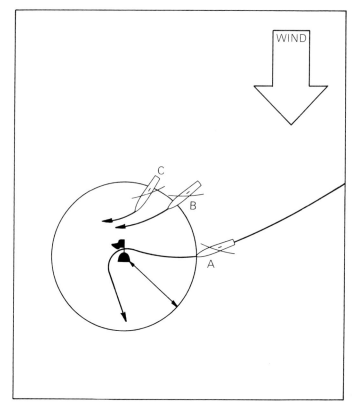

9

A has an overlap and right of way at the mark
B must give A room, and C must give them both room

Skilful gybing:
The last of the group benefits when the leader makes the same mistake, and gains two places with a quick tight gybe. The second board defends his place, in that he can at least cut inside the previous leader

Scrummage at the reaching mark. The inside position matters here! ▷

A   B   C

D

E

A

*Rounding the leeward mark
(left to right, from top):*

Although G65 has gybed already, he has to give room to the board following because the latter established an overlap before reaching the distance of two boards' lengths from the mark.

C

B

*The middle board leaves so much room
between himself and the mark that the third one
nips into the gap by gybing on the spot, and
gains two places*

D

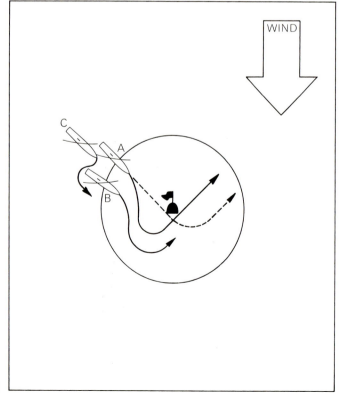

The leeward mark during the World Championships in Florida
The Alpha board (left) has already gybed, hoping to reach the mark before the throng of others with right of way – and succeeds

patches warn of approaching gusts, while small foam crests indicate that a stronger wind is on the way. One's nearby competitors also reveal information, and their sails fortell variations in wind and wave conditions, so that measures can be taken to make good use of them. If the wind is not strong enough for surfing or planing, and fluctuates considerably in strength, luff up in the lulls and bear away in the gusts in order to increase board speed.

Rounding the lee mark follows after the second reach has been sailed, and it is important that it should

A has the inside position and does not drop downwind after the mark (as he would if he sailed along the dotted line).
B has to give room to A. C has no overlap on B, and must keep clear

B

C

85

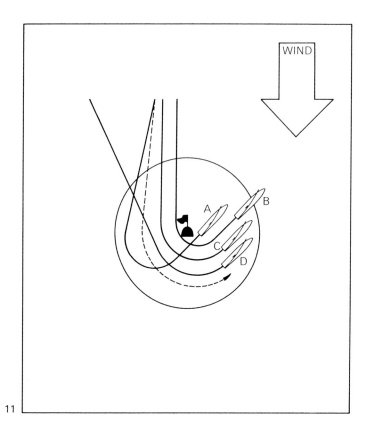

WIND

11

A deliberately lets the others pass, and sails into second place behind B as a result of rounding the mark perfectly

leeward is only able to go about when it can keep clear of other boards that are following behind.

Should you fail to get into the position where you are the inside board of a bunch, remember that you can always slow down just before the mark so that you drop back. You will find from experience that the majority of boards will sag downwind of the mark, leaving a gap in which you will then be able to point up and so start the beat without having lost any ground to leeward (Fig. 11).

The Second Beat

Most of the tactical manoeuvres relevant to the initial upwind leg apply again to the second beat.

The difference from the first beat, however, is that an order has already been established before the lee mark is reached. There is not the same congestion as there was at the start, of course, and there will be a considerable distance between the first and last boards.

Always make as much tactical use as possible of experience gained earlier, and observations made during the race up to this point; for example, did you decide during the first beat that you had chosen the wrong side of the course? If other conditions are unaltered, try not to repeat this or other errors, and gain places by making the necessary corrections. If on the other hand you hardly made any mistakes on the initial beat, check, by careful observation, whether the strategy chosen before still seems equally promising.

To take a slightly closer look at some points: if you are leading and the fleet is well spread out, be careful to avoid a situation that would take you too close to the boards that are still on the reaching legs. Just as when the fleet is closely packed at the start, a line of boards behind or alongside one another affects the strength of the wind, as well as deflecting it.

Another mistake seen frequently is that the starboard tack made to try to get a clear wind is too short. If you go about again too quickly onto port tack, you may find yourself unable to avoid the dirty wind area where other competitors are sailing in line astern of each other towards the mark. You will then be unable to point so well, and will sag slowly to leeward.

be rounded properly because you again need a good starting position from which to set off on the second beat. During the last half of the second reach, it is basically a question of trying to get the inside position at the mark, and if you succeed in this you must take advantage of your position by rounding the mark correctly. If it is clear that you will be inside board before you reach the area stipulated in the Racing Rules of two board's lengths from the mark, you can try to get the other competitors to give you room (Fig. 10), because your board should already be closehauled when you are rounding the mark so that you lose no ground by sagging to leeward. This also leaves less chance of your being blanketed by opponents ahead of you.

If you manage to be as far windward as possible when you round the mark, you have another advantage in that you are free to tack at any time after rounding it, whereas a board that has sagged to

Racing downwind

The Downwind Leg

The run gives boardsailors a lot to think about. So far as technique alone is concerned it is the most difficult point of sailing, but you will find that there are opportunities, frequently unrecognized, by which you can improve your place. On rounding the weather mark your first aim should be to avoid being blanketed by other competitors, because it is on the run that the fleet tends to bunch up, with those at the back catching up on the leaders as a result of the very large area of disturbed wind downwind of their sails. Furthermore, the space that was established between the boards on the water during the beat becomes smaller, due to the fact that in almost all conditions there is a marked reduction in board speed. In such a case, differences in speed are decisive.

A is not afraid of being blanketed and chooses the direct course

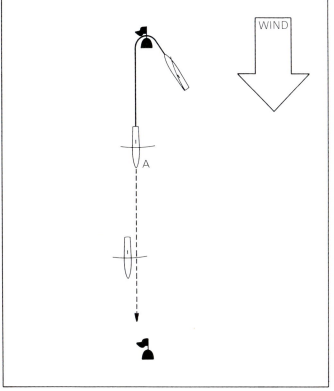

12

When the wind is steady, it is best to choose the direct course to the mark, provided your situation is such that you do not expect any interference from being blanketed by other boards. What is important is to concentrate on avoiding making errors in technique. Problems arise when you find yourself one of a crowd, because everybody has the same aim which is to get clear wind, and often they do so by sailing farther to windward. This inevitably means covering a greater distance, and one is not compensated for this by sailing faster. There is a large area of disturbed wind when boards bunch together like this, and if the majority choose this course, which takes them to windward of the direct line, it can be beneficial to bear away smartly, or to gybe soon after rounding the mark in order to be sure of getting into clear wind. If many others are close astern, do not gybe immediately after rounding because your wind will be adversely affected by boards that are still approaching and roundng the mark.

A constant wind, steady in direction and strength, is the exception rather than the rule. Like other sailing craft, a sailboard is slower when sailing dead before the wind than when on a broad reach, and it therefore pays to make use of minor wind shifts so as to broad reach while keeping as close as possible to the direct course (Fig. 14).

As to variations in the wind's strength, the same tactical considerations apply downwind as on the reaching legs. When there is a lull you should point rather closer to the wind and then, when sailing faster in the gusts, you can try to bear away beyond the direct course to the mark. It is necessary for every racing boardsailor to train with a partner so as to find out for himself what is the right compromise between sailing the direct course more slowly on a dead run, and sailing a broad reach faster while covering a greater distance in the process.

In light to moderate winds, there is no great difficulty in gybing. On the contrary, when the breeze is light you can gybe repeatedly so as to propel the board with vigorous swinging movements of the sail. In a moderate wind, however, although there is no risk when gybing, there is always a slight loss of speed. In stronger winds, when there is a danger that you may

A gybes so as to get away from the rest, and gets a clear wind as quickly as he can

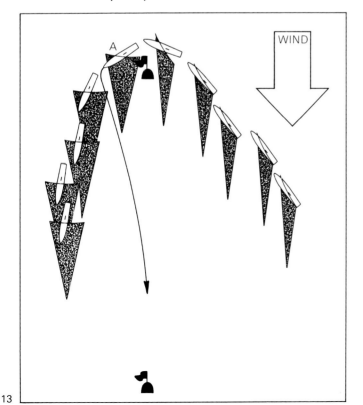

A makes good use of wind shifts, and broad-reaches almost along the direct course to the leeward mark

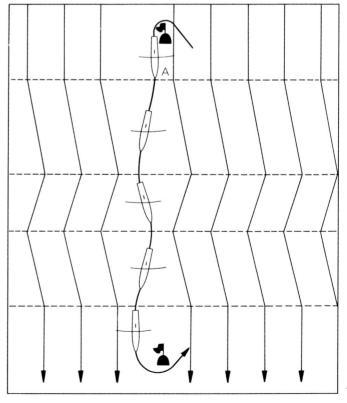

*The Thai sailor Bamroong running downwind
with his daggerboard pulled right out*

drop the sail – or worse – it is a question of weighing up the advantage that could be gained against the risk that comes with every additional gybe. When it is blowing hard, it is often preferable to select a course that can be sailed safely, and to avoid making errors while doing so, rather than to take unnecessary risks, but your decision must depend on the tactics of the moment. If there is a real chance of improving your placing you can 'attack', especially if your points total would not suffer, or if the person following you is far astern and you yourself are hard on the heels of those ahead. Whatever the weather conditions, however, you must be sure that you will be in a favourable position when rounding the leeward mark, that is as the inside board. In moderate and strong winds, do not gybe just before reaching the mark because it has been proved that the psychological stress increases when you are anticipating rounding a mark. Many people find that it is more difficult to bear away for the mark after gybing when there is only a very short distance left in which to do so. The same basic rules apply when rounding the leeward mark as were already described for the mark at the end of the broad reach.

Particular attention should be paid to making use of the waves when running. The direct course to the mark rarely pays in a seaway, first because the waves are generally shorter than the length of the board and the bow tends to dive beneath the waves, and second because the waves usually slip under the board without accelerating it. The important thing in using waves is to be able to pick out a good one on which the board will be able to surf for a period. When you have spotted such a wave, you accelerate by luffing up gently, simultaneously tilting the board to leeward. When the wave has almost reached the stern, try to match the speed of the wave by quickly sheeting the rig in several times (pumping).

Your aim is to stay sailing down the face of the wave for as long as possible, but if you are on a dead run the board will sail straight down the wave face and be braked by the wave ahead, the unfortunate effect of which is that you cannot immediately get the board going at full speed again and the wave will slip beneath it. You can avoid this by sailing a course that is almost a broad reach, the angle of the course to the waves depending on the speed of your board: if you slow down, steer more directly down the wave face, but if your speed increases steer along the wave. The extra distance that you sail to the mark as a result of using waves in this way is almost always made up for by the increase in speed, which can be as high as 30 per cent.

With regard to the recommendation to 'pump' to increase speed, it has to be said that you would be wise to try to discover the race officers' attitude to this. Difficulties and unpleasantness result whenever a breach of the rules is disputed, and many officials therefore tend to ignore the problem, but be cautious if race officers are known to adopt a hard line over pumping – particularly if observers are patrolling the broad-reaching and running legs in small boats. There is little hope of success when it comes to fighting a disqualification for pumping.

The Final Beat, and Finishing the Race

Apart from any protests that may have occurred, it is not until the finishing line has been crossed that a race is over, and every competitor should remember this fact. All too frequently one can observe lack of concentration or a resigned attitude resulting in further places being lost on the final beat. It often helps to counter this psychologically by thinking 'I am out here anyway – at least I can try.' Even when the situation is hopeless it is worth trying a long shot to make up lost ground by sailing right out to one side of the course.

You must plan your tactics for the finishing beat before you start the leg, however, and when deciding on your strategy you must take the actions of other competitors more into account than on the previous windward legs.

If you are leading with a board close astern, and a third rather farther back, you should play safe and not try to make use of a wind shift by tacking on it, unless the sailor close astern of you tacks too. A person lying second, on the other hand, should try to get clear of the leader so that he is able to sail into the lead if he gets a fortunate wind shift. Provided that the third board is not followed closely by another, he can take a long tack right away from the first two boards, hoping to win the race himself if the wind shifts in his favour.

If you are forced into defending a place, you should cover your opponent by going about every time he goes about. To do this, try to sail directly to windward of him, preferably in such a way that you can watch him through the window in the sail and react immediately to every move he makes. But be careful if you find yourself battling closely with him, because short tacks made too frequently will allow other boards that are father astern to benefit from your pre-occupation with your private duel and your reduced average speeds. It it very rare that it pays you to defend your place against one board while you simultaneously allow four others to pass you.

Naturally there are also situations when, with the total points for the series in mind, you base your tactics, not on being first over the line, but on concentrating on beating a particular rival. If you are in second place on total points for a series with no bad result to discard, while the boardsailor in first place is leading as a result

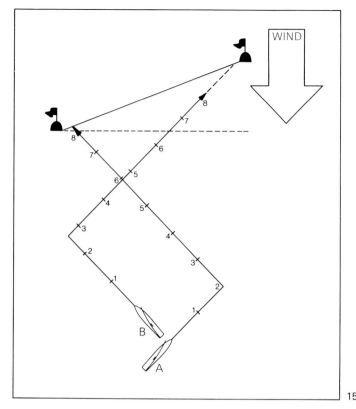

A beats B by choosing to finish at the better end of the line

of discarding one poor result, it is absolutely legitimate to cover him very closely so as to try to make him lose a number of places.

There are many tactical opportunities when making for the finishing line. Although this should be laid at 90° to the wind direction, this is rarely the case in practice and the consequence could be that a board-sailor, in spite of having worked his board farther to windward than his immediate rival, will finish behind him (Fig. 15).

As is the problem when tacking for the windward mark, it is a question of going about at the right place and moment, so as to sail for the line with right of way on starboard tack. If you are sailing over to this place on part tack from the left side of the course, and are forced into giving way to opponents sailing on starboard tack, you should willingly pass astern of them so as to be in a strong position tactically at the finishing line (Fig. 16).

Open regatta in ideal weather

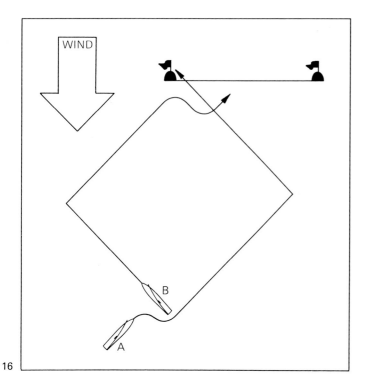

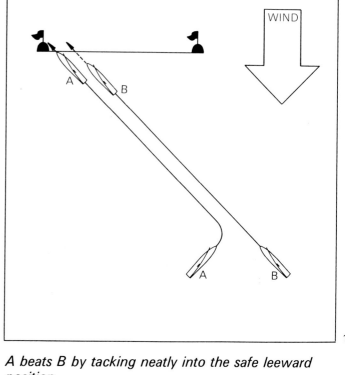

A beats B by passing astern of him, to be in a better tactical position for the finish

A beats B by tacking neatly into the safe leeward position

Another situation when it pays to give away a little ground by sailing past your opponent's stern is when you can lay the finishing line while he still has to go about again. This will almost certainly take him more time than you will take to make good the little ground you have lost, because you will partly compensate for that with your increased speed. If your opponent is able to lay the finishing mark you should attack by going about close to leeward of him, to get into the safe leeward position where you stay, slowing him down with your dirty wind, right up to the finishing line (Fig. 17). This is why the best course, when on starboard tack, is when you are just able to lay the finishing mark, and can fetch it without having to tack again. If neither of two boards on starboard tack can fetch the finishing mark, the one to windward can delay making the last task until he has a shorter distance to sail to the finish (Fig. 18).

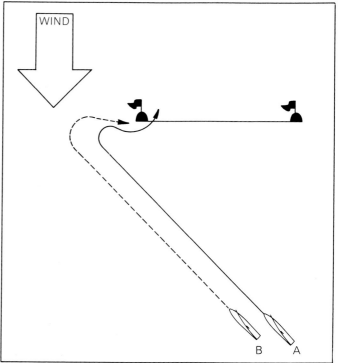

A does not let B tack, but takes him beyond the mark. B then has a greater distance to sail back to the finish line.

EQUIPMENT
Theory of Sails

Before a class championship

Aerodynamics

Even someone who is just starting to learn windsurfing will understand immediately why it is that a board (or a boat) can sail downwind. It is not only umbrellas and leaves that the wind blows away, but boats and boards as well. When sailing directly downwind the air does not flow over the sail: it acts simply by resisting the wind (Fig. 1). The camber or curvature of the sail is largely irrelevant; all that matters is its area, the way that the board is shaped and the total weight.

It is harder to understand why a board or boat will sail forward when the wind is blowing from the side, and even why it is able to sail at an angle towards the wind. In these cases air flows over and past the sail, and a series of aerodynamic laws comes into force.

Fig. 2 shows the cross-section of a sail with attached airflow (i.e. the flow has not broken away from the sail, causing loss of power). What happens is that some of the air takes the longer route behind the sail, to leeward of it, whereas the air passing on the windward side takes a shorter route. Bernoulli's equation states that the sum of potential energy (static air pressure) and kinetic energy (air in motion) is always the same, and in consequence static air pressure drops when the speed of moving air rises. There is therefore a drop in pressure where air moves faster to leeward of the sail,

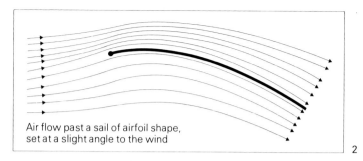

Air flow past a sail of airfoil shape, set at a slight angle to the wind

2

whereas pressure rises to windward where airflow is slower. The faster the air flows over the lee side of the sail, the lower is the pressure there.

The pressure differences at various points on a sail can be found by measurement, and Fig. 3 shows relevant experiment using an airfoil in a wind tunnel. The different levels of the fluid in the manometers show how the reduction in pressure varies across the upper surface of the airfoil. At D1 the pressure ahead of the leading edge is normal. D2 and D3 show clearly how much pressure has dropped, and there is also a reduction at D4. Behind the shape at D5, pressure has returned to normal again, undisturbed by the airfoil. The similar pressure differences that result when air flows over a sail can be shown as a diagram by analysing the reduction in pressure on the lee side and the increase in pressure to windward (Fig. 4).

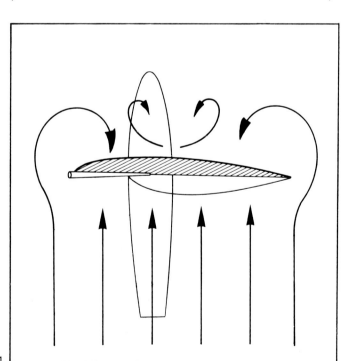

1

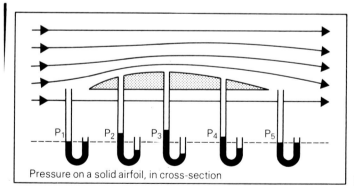

Pressure on a solid airfoil, in cross-section

3

PRESSURE AND FORCE

It is clear that the sum of the reduced pressures to leeward is markedly greater than that of the increased pressures to windward. So far as the boardsailor is concerned, this diagram is informative because he can see that power is greater on the lee side of the sail. He must therefore pay greater attention to airflow to leeward, and try to find the optimum angle of the sail to

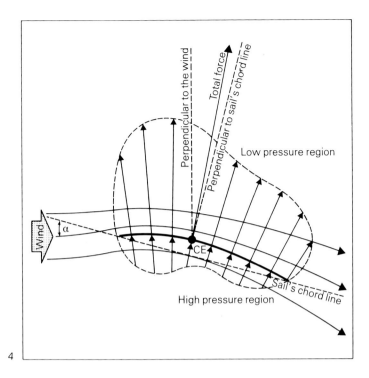

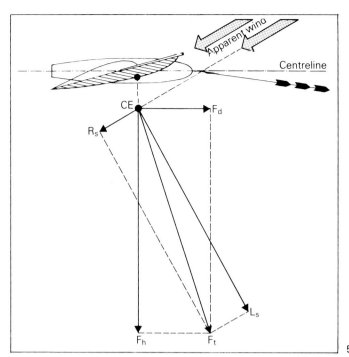

the wind (angle of attack) while being particularly careful to avoid obstructing airflow over the lee side of the sail. The mast also causes a reduction in the power of any sail, not so much because of its own air resistance but because it affects airflow over the sail in such a way that there is a lesser reduction in pressure at the forward part of the sail, and thus less force (or lift) there. This is why it is advisable to use as slim a mast as possible so that maximum drive can be obtained from the sail.

FORCES ON THE SAIL AND BOARD

The sail, the sailor and the board all slow down the wind when it arrives, and the first effect on it is simply that of resistance, or drag, which is the same thing as the resistance that results when a car or bicycle are in motion. Drag (R_s) is relatively small in the case of the sail. When air flows over the sail as already described the result is a force called lift (L_s) which acts at right angles to the direction of the apparent wind. Total force (F_t) is the resultant of the parallelogram of forces made up of resistance or drag and lift (Fig. 5).

The forces named above are those that relate to the sail itself, removed from the board. If no other forces were involved, the wind would drive board and sail in

the direction of total force, but in reality F_t is opposed by a counter force that arises from the underwater body of the sailboard, namely from the immersed part of the board plus the streamlined daggerboard and skeg. The forces produced by the sail are transmitted down to the board through the sailor's arms, legs and feet, and also via the mast and mast step.

When the total force (F_t) is considered as the resultant of forces acting on the board, its components are the two forces which arise when the board resists being driven sideways in the direction of F_t. These are the driving component F_d, which thrusts the board forward, and then the considerably greater sideways force F_h, which pushes it to leeward, and which is opposed by the immersed edge of the sailboard, the skeg(s) and the daggerboard. Both parallelograms of forces are shown in Fig. 5.

The foregoing explanation clearly relates to a board that is sailing close to the wind; when sailing farther off the wind the proportion of side force is reduced, while driving force is increased.

The steering mechanics of a sailboard operate by means of the forces just described. In the case of a normal sailing boat, these forces have to cancel each other out if the craft is to stay on course without suffering from the braking effect of a rudder held over continuously to one side. A sailboard also will only sail in a straight line when the total aerodynamic force is in equilibrium with the total hydrodrynamic force, but the rig can be raked farther forward or aft at will to create a particular condition of imbalance, and Fig. G shows the various conditions that can exist:

a. Here the line of action of total sail force through the centre of effort (CE) of the sail is farther aft than that of the centre of lateral resistance (CLR) or total hull force, and this causes the board to turn up into the wind.
b. This shows the condition when both forces are in equilibrium and act nearly along a single line. The board sails straight on a steady course.
c. Here the rig has been raked forward so that the force developed by the sail acts ahead of the hydrodynamic force, and the board bears away from the wind.

Another important force that affects the steering of a sailboard is the torque which results when the centre of effort of the sail (CE) does not lie vertically above the hull's centre of lateral resistance (CLR). It is not only total force F_t that acts on the sail at the CE, but the forces of which it is composed. The farther the sail is out to leeward, the farther outboard does driving force F_d act, and this causes a rotational effect between the hull and the rig's drive acting to leeward, which makes the board luff up (Fig. 7). This effect is particularly noticeable when beginners are struggling to start and get under way.

However, when the wind is strong the normal sailing position is very different. The boardsailor pulls the rig well over to windward, and increases the torque resulting from the position of the centre of gravity of his body. The effect is that total aerodynamic force does not act on the sail in a horizontal direction but upwards, and the consequence is that the sail carries part of the sailor's weight. At the same time torque is making the board bear away because the force F_t is acting outboard again, through the CE which, this time, is to windward. When sailing in a strong wind, the effect can be so great that the rig has to be raked far

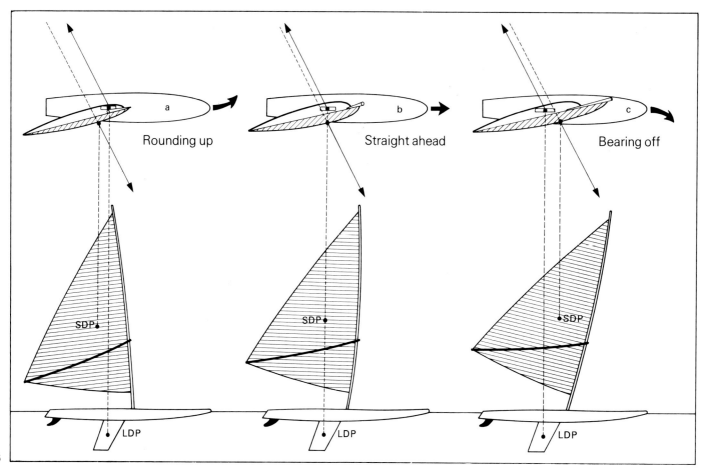

6

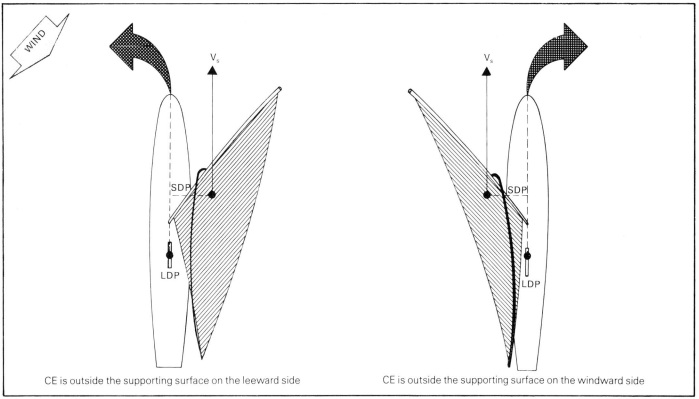

CE is outside the supporting surface on the leeward side

CE is outside the supporting surface on the windward side

back to keep the board sailing straight; in other words, the CE has to be moved further aft so that its position relative to the CLR is where the rotational effect of driving force is cancelled out.

If the board is to be able to sail at optimum speed, the aim is to keep driving force F_d, which is directed forward, as great as possible, while all resistance, including side force F_h, is reduced to the minimum.

SAIL FULLNESS

When the aerodynamic performance of a curved sail is compared to that of a flat plate, it is very evident that it is the curved sail which produces greater drive. The secret of the increase in drive lies in the curvature of the sail.

What, then, is the optimum fullness or camber for windsurfing sails? Fig. 8, a profile sketched over a photo of sail, shows an American method by which camber can roughly be determined. Here the distance between the leading edge and the position of maximum camber, and the measurement of the maximum

depth of camber, are expressed as percentages of the length of the chord across the sail at that particular level, and these figures enable at least a rough description and evaluation to be made of the sail shape. The shape of the curve is not defined, however.

The fuller the sail, the greater is the total lift or force it generates, but only up to a certain point. F_t acts in a direction that is directed progressively less forward and more sideways as fullness increases, owing to the fact that the driving force component of the parallelogram of forces increases less than proportionately. Matters are complicated also by the fact that higher wind speed tends to push the fullness back towards the leech, also increasing the undesirable sideways element in the total force (Fig. 4). In light airs, a full sail is often fast, however.

One of the problems when a sail is very full is that the area just forward of the leech is very rounded. Suction on the leeward side, resulting from the pressure difference already mentioned, acts at right angles to the surface of the sail (Fig. 4) and this has a braking effect near the leech. Sails with fullness near the leech are consequently always slow. Another problem is that the boardsailor has to transmit to the board the greater total

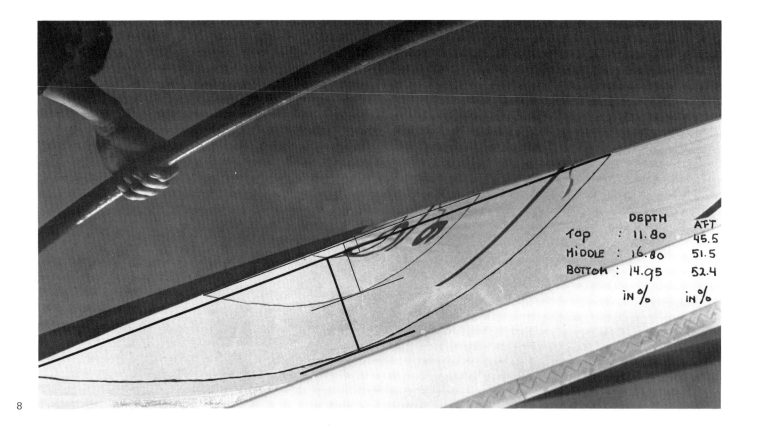

DEPTH | AFT
Top : 11.80 | 45.5
MIDDLE : 16.80 | 51.5
BOTTOM : 14.95 | 52.4
in % | in %

8

force produced by a sail with larger camber, and even a very strong sailor can only do this in light to moderate breezes; when the wind is stronger such a sail will be too powerful. Variation of wind speeds must therefore also be taken into consideration, and sail camber must be a compromise.

Fig. 8 shows the camber across different sections of a sail in a force 2 breeze. With little tension on the sail, the belly (maximum fullness) lies slightly forward and the profile is rounded at the leech.

Maximum camber for a sailboard's light weather sail is about 13 to 15 per cent of chord length (the chord being the straight-line distance from luff to leech), and the position of maximum camber between 43 and 45 per cent of chord length. When winds are heavier maximum camber should be about 10 per cent, and the position of the belly no farther back than 45 per cent of the chord length. If the forward part of a sail is too rounded, and maximum camber too far forward, at say under 40 per cent, the sail will not be able to draw at as small an angle to the wind as would one with the position of maximum camber at mid-chord length; while a sail with maximum camber nearer the leech than 55 per cent of chord length will suffer from the

same braking effect as was described above in connection with the closed leech.

When camber is considered vertically, the first point is that, from the head to the foot of the sail, the position of maximum camber should stay at about the same percentage of chord lengths back from the luff. Second, camber should increase with height above the foot, and only flatten near the head. Good vertical distribution for a sailboard's sail would be about 12 per cent camber at wishbone boom level, increasing gradually to 14 per cent and then decreasing near the head to 13 per cent of horizontal chord lengths.

It is important to make a close inspection of a sail, looking upwards as shown here, to be able to form an opinion as to its characteristics by checking the position and degree of maximum camber.

The fullness of all sailboard sails should be such that they do not touch the wishbone when wind pressure is strong. There is a very damaging effect on the power produced by a sail when it is split into two by the boom,

An up-to-date funboard sail with a fully battened 'fathead'

because pressure increases greatly with little contribution being made to forward drive. Another essential, of course, is that the boom should be strong enough not to bend when it takes the weight of the sailor hanging outboard, because the length of a boom decreases as it bends and lets the sail become so much fuller that it is liable to be divided into two parts where it presses against the boom. The additional fullness of the lower part of the sail would also increase side force, rather than boosting driving force.

MYLAR vs DACRON/TERYLENE

Although great importance is attached to the total weight of a board, a factor which is watched very carefully, relatively little attention is paid to the weight of the mast and of the sail. This attitude is utterly wrong. Not only does the rig represent a large proportion of the total weight of a sailboard, but owing to its height the rig exerts a considerable moment which has the effect of multiplying its effective weight.

As sail material, Mylar has a number of advantages by comparison with Terylene or Dacron. It is lighter in weight, owing to its being strong; and in spite of the fact that it is considerably less thick, the material can be used to make sails that do not stretch, and therefore do not lose their shape. Mylar film also takes up very little water when immersed, and that is another reason why sails made from this material are lighter to use than more water-absorbent sailcloth. These simple advantages are obvious, but another is that, with Mylar, camber can be put in by cutting very accurately. When tested for elongation Mylar film excels due to its resistance to stretching. This means that, whereas with a conventional synthetic fibre sail stretch has to be taken into account when it is designed and cut, because the sail becomes fuller when under load and also the position of maximum camber shifts aft, with a Mylar sail it is possible to cut the cloth with the exact camber that is required and the fullness will stay virtually unaltered when under greater pressure. A Mylar sail can therefore be cut to the optimum shape from the start, and without having to allow for the differences in stretch that exist along the length and width of woven cloth.

How well a sail will keep its shape is determined by the stretch factor of the cloth used, and sailmakers nowadays can obtain three broad types of sailcloth with low, medium or high stretch factors. All woven cloth stretches more when pulled on the bias (dia-gonally across its woven shape), and in the case of light cloth with a high stretch factor the bias stretch is six times greater than the weft stretch. (In weaving the weft thread runs *across* the cloth, not lengthwise.) When wind pressure increases such sail cloth stretches diagonally along the bias: the sail becomes fuller, the shape of its camber changes, and the position of maximum camber moves farther aft. Such sailcloth is suitable only for light winds.

One side of medium and low stretch sailcloth is impregnated with a filler after weaving, and this keeps the stretch ratio down to 1:2. Such sailcloth holds its shape considerably better than the stretchier light-weather cloth, and sail camber is maintained more readily.

At present time it is Mylar, with its 1:1 stretch ratio, that keeps its shape most satisfactorily, and the importance of maintaining the camber that is cut into a sail is best shown by the following example.

In a strong wind, the material of a sail that is 6 metres square and made of high stretch sailcloth, will stretch 5–10 cm. It is true that bending the mast more will partly offset this, but an increase in the length between mast and clew of as little as 2 cm will increase the fullness of the sail by over 5 per cent. That is enough for a sail with a 15 per cent camber, which produces driving force efficiently, to become one with 20 per cent or more camber, and that is unsuitable for a strong wind. The effect is the same if the gap between the two booms widens, thus effectively reducing the length of the booms and the length from mast to clew on the sail.

When cloth has a high stretch factor, the luff of the sail at the mast has to be under considerably greater tension than if the sailcloth resists stretch, and that means that the degree of mast bend must be much greater, which in turn makes the sail flatter. Consequently the sail will only become fuller when wind pressure is sufficiently high, and the result is that the all-round performance of such a sail suffers on account of being under so much tension that it is too flat, both when the wind is light and when wind pressure is too low on the runs and reaches; a full-cut sail will then be superior.

The heavily tensioned leech of a sail cut from cloth with a high stretch factor behaves as if it was set on a stay, and barely adjusts when pressure on the sail increases on the beat. The sail is prevented from reacting naturally by twisting and releasing pressure, as would a less stretchy sail that is under less tension. Twist in the sail and the release of pressure makes the rig easier to handle, and enables the board to sail faster.

The ideal: sail and mast are well matched, with the luff round cut to suit the flexibility of the mast. Camber is fully effective

A bad match. A sail cut for a stiff mast is here set on a flexible one. The stronger bend thus put into it has caused creasing, running to the clew from where mast bend is excessive.

THE MAST AND SAIL AS A UNIT

It is not only the stretchiness of sailcloth but the question of how stiff the mast should be that has to be answered. The rig can only be considered in its entirety, a unit that is made up of mast and sail. If a sail made of low stretch sailcloth and cut for use with a stiff mast is set on a more flexible mast, heavy creasing is bound to occur where the mast bends more than the sailmaker allowed for when he cut the sail, as illustrated here.

Assuming that sail trim is normal, the way a more flexible mast bends backwards and sideways will change greatly as the wind varies, and the sailmaker cannot therefore cut into the sail a specific luff round that is suitable for all conditions. One answer is to use extreme tension for such a rig, because the degree of mast bend can then be controlled better, and if mast and sail are set up in this way they will be quite functional in a strong wind but not particularly fast. The extreme tension prevents the mast from sagging too far to leeward.

Medium stiff epoxy/glassfibre masts or really stiff aluminium masts are noticeably better. In winds of up to moderate strength a medium stiff epoxy mast can be used successfully; when the wind is moderate, and sideways bend is not so marked, the epoxy mast has the same bending characteristics as an aluminium mast. In a strong wind, however, the medium stiff epoxy mast yields to the greater wind pressure by bending out to leeward and aft. This causes the sail to twist so much that the camber which provides forward drive is lost because the leech sags away to leeward.

A stiff aluminium mast with a sail made of low stretch cloth would fully convert all these forces, and the result would be a notable increase in drive owing to the control of leech twist. There would of course always be a reduction in area, and this is a good example of the fact that a sail that is smaller in area but has good camber will produce greater drive than a larger sail with a distorted profile.

PROFILE SHAPE

It is easy to state what makes a successful sail: it is one which produces most drive from a given area. In the end, that really only means that the actual area of the sail is of secondary importance. Naturally a sailmaker can easily cut a very large sail which is entirely flat so that it can be handled easily in spite of its size, but such a sail will not produce as much drive as its area warrants; also its drag would be excessive, and it would be slower than a smaller, fuller sail.

The all-round sail used formerly, a simple triangular sail sometimes with a hollow leech, is an unhandy, ineffective sail that is less powerful than a smaller sail cut with fullness based on up-to-date knowledge. The first rule is that a sail needs to have battens along the leech, so that the fullness will taper aft smoothly. A sail without battens always has an unstable leech, and the shape of the after part is uncontrolled. It is when wind increases that the leech roach, supported by the battens, twists the sail as is required to relieve the load on the sailor.

The second rule is that less drive and more side force are produced by a shorter wider sail than by a taller narrower one. A consequence of this is the shorter wishbone boom. Today's 'fathead' sails are extra wide near the head with a full-length batten high up; they also have a generous leech roach and relatively short booms. The leech is therefore relatively short too, and this makes it possible to counter outward rotation by pulling the sail far to windward of the centreline. The short boom also makes it considerably easier to tack and gybe, and the whole rig handles better.

Tuning Tips

Division II (Open Class) displacement boards are highly developed racing designs and optimum tuning is part of the technical perfection required to master and get the best from them.

In the widest sense, the tuning of a racing board could be said to start with the choice of the board and with its maintenance, because a displacement board is designed purely as a racing machine. It is just as sensitive as a 470 racing dinghy, and demands equally careful treatment.

Some sort of cover, even wrapping in plastic sheet, should be used when the sailboard is being stored or transported, so as to keep the board, and its underwater surface in particular, free from grease and dirt as well as providing some protection against knocks, scratching and other damage. If you have to manage without, it is advisable to clean the underwater and edge surfaces regularly, perhaps even rubbing them down with fine sandpaper. Even a film of grease considerably increases frictional resistance.

The careful preparation of the fin (skeg) and daggerboard could also be considered to be part of maintenance. Ridges are usually left at the leading and trailing edges of factory-made moulded components, and they are often only partly removed. Such ridges immediately disturb the flow of water, and it is therefore important to take the 'brake' off with a file, finishing the edges by rubbing down with sandpaper.

Racing boards and daggerboard blades are easily damaged or scratched and must be protected while travelling, e.g. before a flight, even if it means in your sleeping bag.

So far as the fin is concerned, it must be said that, although most of the polyester ones are prettily coloured, they are poorly streamlined, the manufacturers often being content merely to taper them to a greater or lesser extent at the trailing and leading edges. Currently the best fins are those made by the injection moulding process. They are fully streamlined, and are also strong enough from top to bottom. On the shorter planing boards the purpose of the fin is to provide directional stability, but longer racing sailboards are inherently more directionally stable owing to the shape of the displacement hull, and large fins are therefore unnecessary. On the contrary, it is a question of having a small fin so as to retain good manoeuvrability.

The daggerboard needs equally careful attention. Too early a separation of water flow from the surface has even worse consequences then in the case of the skeg, and tests have proved that even the slightest roughness of the surface causes turbulence.

Care is required to see that there is no gap either side where a daggerboard that is raised and lowered vertically protrudes through the bottom of the sailboard. There are fewer ways in which a sailboard can be tuned and its balance adjusted if it has a dag-

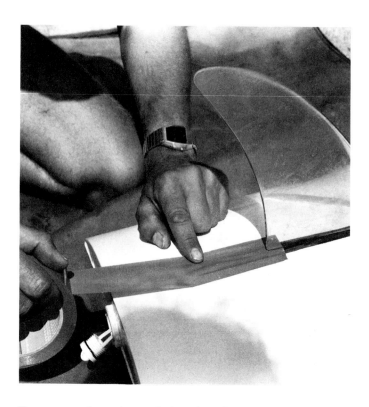

Tape over the edges of the skeg box

Sand off the ridge on the front of the skeg

The sealing strip reduces drag produced by turbulence over the long slot

Pivoting swing-back centreboard, infinitely adjustable while under way

gerboard of this type, rather than a pivoting type (properly called a centreboard), but it is important to ensure that it will stay where you want it, down or partly raised in a number of different positions.

The Mistral M1 has a swing-back fully retracting centreboard, which can be adjusted by foot. The pivot point is high up, and when the centreboard is raised it is mostly stowed inside the hull, while flexible strips make the underside of the case watertight along the slot. In the Pan Am Cup, the first ten boards had this sort of centreboard case. The blade area protruding beneath the hull can be reduced to whatever extent is required by pivoting the centreboard with one foot. With regard to the board's sailing characteristics in strong winds, the important point to note is that the centre of lateral resistance shifts farther aft when the angle of incidence increases as a centreboard is angled back. Only a small part protrudes below the bottom of the hull when it is raised as far as it will go, and this is enough to enable the sailor to keep control of the board, especially when reaching. The same system has proved effective with the Mistral Tandem.

The angle of incidence of the centreboards fitted to most racing sailboards is 10°, and assuming that the draft with it lowered is 70 cm which is the maximum draft permitted, this means that closehauled performance is very good. Leverage becomes so great, however, that there is a tendency for the board to capsize easily. In a strong wind, when one sheets in the sail closehauled it will feel as though the board is increasingly ready to capsize, and this will happen to lightweight sailors at slower wind speeds than it does to heavyweights.

There are three ways in which you can avoid capsizing. As far as possible you should try to keep your weight vertically over the windward edge of the board, and that means sailing in a more or less deep crouch with your arms bent. On no account should you lean far back and sail with outstretched arms when it is blowing hard. Second, you must try to sail right on the limit of capsizing, with the board pointing really close

Karl Messmer sailing a 'sinker'. Obviously an efficient sail is especially important here. ▷▷

to the wind so that the angle of incidence of the water streaming past is kept very small; you keep the sail open, ready to be let out slightly with your sail hand to spill wind. Should the board still threaten to capsize, you can increase the angle of incidence of the centreboard by raking it about 5° to 10° farther aft, and you will then be able to harden the sail right in again.

It is when reaching and running, however, that the advantages of this type of pivoting centreboard are really decisive. Can anyone have failed to turn a board over when sailing down a wave with no pressure in the sail? It is possible to adjust the angle and exposed area of blade to match the strength of the wind in such a way that the board is discouraged from capsizing and remains reasonably stable.

It is the rig that really decides how fast the board will sail; after all it is the power source. A stiff epoxy and glassfibre mast, or better still a tapered aluminium mast with a stiff wishbone boom, is essential in order to

Centreboard case sealed off forward of the retractable blade ▽

The flexible slot seal closes around the centreboard as it pivots back

Correct trapeze line adjustment ▷

Luff tension can be adjusted by the downhaul, held by a Clam cleat at the mast foot

obtain optimum sail shape. An effective method of stretching the luff is to fit a cleat at the mast foot or to incorporate one in the downhaul itself; you can then adjust luff tension as needed during the race, say if the wind drops away suddenly, without having to let go of the rig.

The connection between mast and boom should be as tight as possible so that the rig is rigid; any corrections to sail trim will then be passed directly from the sailor's arms to the whole rig. Another reason why the mast to boom connection should be really tight is because it makes it easier to check and control how taut the outhaul is. A really useful aid for checking the tension of the outhaul is to mark a stripe on each side of the wishbone booms, as well as on both ends of the outhaul line.

Another handy tip enables you to adjust outhaul tension when you are out on the water while the rig is upright. Form a loop about the size of your fist in the outhaul aft of the cleat by tying a bowline, and do this for both ends of the line. To adjust tension on the clew, you briefly grasp the mast above the boom with your mast hand and grab hold of the loop with your sheet hand; you can then either increase or ease tension on the outhaul as necessary. Special boom-end fittings, or even blocks, can be used to reduce friction and make a finer adjustment.

Go for a quick sail shortly before the race and adjust the rig, just as you would when racing a boat. As a rule, sails should be set flatter for a stronger wind than for a light breeze. Increasing luff tension pulls the position of maximum camber farther forward, while tightening the outhaul makes the sail flatter and shifts camber farther aft. (The position of maximum camber has already been discussed.) There are also some basic rules for specific wave conditions. In calm water, when there are no waves, the sail can be flatter so that you are able to point as high as possible. When the wind is moderate and waves are short and steep, the sail should be rather fuller so that it will develop enough drive to keep the board moving well without being stopped by the waves.

In stronger winds, be sure that the sail has enough twist, in other words check that the leech stays open (falls away from the board) near the head of the sail. This is achieved by keeping the outhaul really taut,

Adjusting tension on the sail with the clew outhaul. The loop in the end of the outhaul makes it easy to catch and pull, and keeps the line in the cleat

Two mast sockets for different conditions

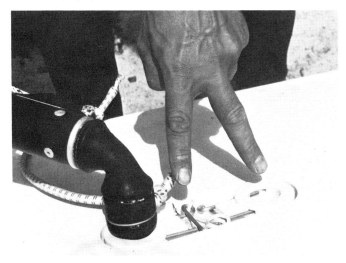

even if a crease appears along the foot. With a modern sail this creasing will not occur because the lowest cloth is cut fuller and is made of doubled sail cloth. A boardsailor who tunes his rig really well can make his sail slightly fuller for the reach and run by easing the tension on the luff and leech.

Most displacement boards have two or more mast foot positions. It is a widely accepted fallacy that shifting the rig from one to the other alters the position of the centre of effort, but in reality it is only the position of the rig and the relationship of the centre of effort to the centre of lateral resistance of the board that alter. The mast is either raked slightly forward, or stands upright.

Figure-of-eight knot made around the line to form a loop

The loop pulled tight

The forward mast socket should be the better in principle, because a more upright mast is preferable for aerodynamic reasons. It is only when the wind is strong (force 5 and above) that the after position is better, and there are two reasons for this. The first is that stepping the rig farther aft when the board is sailing fast brings the rig closer to the CLR which itself also shifts farther aft. Second, a problem would otherwise arise because, when the daggerboard has been entirely removed or raised fully and the rig raked far back, the end of the boom would trail in the water.

A trapeze harness is also very useful. It is important to take a deep breath before securing the upper strap, so that it will not constrict your chest later on.

There are a number of patent methods of attaching the trapeze lines with elaborate cleats or fabric straps. The following is a simple but practicable solution. In the short line, led under the boom, tie a figure-of-eight knot around the long end, which will not slip out if you tie a simple overhand knot in the end of it. The advantage of this is that both knots can be opened easily, shifted and tightened again.

It is particularly important that the position where the lines are attached to the boom should match the wind strength, and the rule is that the more wind there is the farther aft the lines should be. They should be tied in such a way that the pull of the sail does not come on the hook alone, but lightly on the sail hand as well. For a racing sailboard, the lines should be of such a length that they are attached a good metre apart along the boom; the position that you chose before the start can then be changed in whatever way is necessary during the race. The distance one stands from the boom should be such that your arms are slightly bent when you hang out, and you will then be able to correct sail trim continuously with your arms without having to move your body at all.

There are many arguments for and against using a harness. It is permitted in Division II and, quite apart from saving strength, the great advantage is that the rig can be kept much quieter than when arms alone are used. The boardsailor's arms are then free to deal mainly with fine corrections to sail trim and mast rake.

Funboards

Funboards only race in force 4 or over

The sport of board racing has recently extended to new types of competition. For some time almost all European board manufacturers based their new de-

signs on the norms and conditions of the Open Class, but parallel development has now started. The standard of boardsailing today is so much higher that there is a marked decrease in the interest in merely being able to stand up on a board in light winds, and it is not until wind strengths are over force 4 that the real meaning of the word 'windsurfing' can be appreciated. Footstraps, harnesses and a more dynamic technique are characteristic of this trend. Funboards are sailboards which have been designed for strong wind specialists, and there is a big difference between their types. The short ones, 2.5 to 3.3 metres long, are designed only for use in breaking waves or surf, and are suitable for wave sailing and jumping. The longer funboards are about 3.5 to 3.9 metres in length, and their advanced design and construction as all-round boards makes them suitable for strong wind sailing. They have a pivoting or fully retracting daggerboard and, unlike the short boards, their performance is relatively good when closehauled. It is because this type of funboard is so long, and its longitudinal stability is therefore adequate, that it is still a pleasure to sail in the open sea when it is really choppy.

Fins on short and long funboards

Different funboards

114

Possible footstrap arrangements

Although the first World Cup was to take place in Hawaii in 1978, the long funboards did not really make an impact until the Pan Am World Cup series in 1980, which was held in winds of force 5 to 7 and waves up to 5 metres high. The Hawaiian sailors have had plenty of experience of strong winds, and they have been prominent in the development of equipment.

Early attempts to race in surf were not very successful, but 1981 saw the first Euro-Funboard Cup series. This provided for a combination of five series of races, each run in one of the best European strong wind areas, and even though the actual number of races was sometimes fewer than planned, at least some races were run in the right conditions at each venue.

Reaching leg, during the Pan Am Cup in Hawaii. In the background is the most famous, if not infamous, reaching mark in the world, Birdshit Rock ▷▷

Fully retracting or 'vario' centreboard on a long
racing design

Funboards gybing

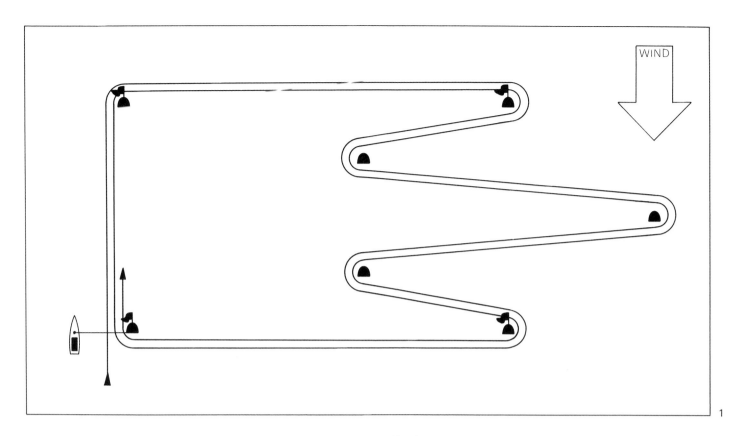

Adjustable mast step and foot-operated centreboard

Funboard course: not much beating, a lot of beam and broad reaching, and ten gybes

Funboards are usually started in two classes; in the Construction Class there are no restrictions whatsoever, whereas in the Open Class the number of sails and minimum board weight are limited.

So as to be sure that the boards will achieve high speeds, the course is selected with a greater proportion of beam-reaching and broad-reaching than of beating. A short beat is essential, however, so that the start will be orderly and allows one line to serve for start and finish. The diagram shows a typical funboard course.

The Construction Class is the more interesting of the two, from the tactical aspect. Because there is absolute freedom of choice as to gear, the first tactical decisions have to be made while the sailor is still on land. The design of planing flat boards enables them to carry a potentially large area of sail, always assuming that the boardsailor is skilful enough to handle it, and it is most difficult to choose which sail to use. If you select too small a sail you run the risk of sailing too slowly to be

Start of the Hawaii marathon race

able to plane, whereas if the sail is too large you could be overpowered and would waste the larger area, losing much of the power which would otherwise be converted into forward drive. It is therefore best to try out the rig beforehand and, preferably, to have two rigs set up ready so that you can exchange them quickly if the wind increases or decreases. Funboard races are almost always run very close to the shore, so that a decision can be left until a few minutes before the start. Your choice will often be affected by what other people have done.

The same holds good when deciding which daggerboard to use. If wind speeds are relatively low, a larger daggerboard is more suitable when it comes to the upwind legs, but its greater wetted area is a disadvantage during the long beam reach and on the broad-reaching legs.

Thorough preparation of all the gear is advisable, and of the footstraps and the surface of the board in particular. Footstraps must not twist, and they must stay standing upright and open rather than dropping flat. Even if footstraps are fitted, it is important for the surface to be non-slip everywhere you may stand when you are not using them, because it is just when you are in the process of some critical manoeuvre such as gybing that you need to place your feet elsewhere.

The distance between two funboards changes much more quickly when a mistake in technique is made than in normal triangle racing, because speeds are higher.

The start of the race is particularly important because the initial beat is so short that there are fewer opportunities to use tactics. The beat must be planned before the start, and it is important to keep the number of tacks to the minimum because it takes a lot of time to put a funboard about; nor will it gain ground to windward, as Open Class boards do, when it is tacked slowly. Exceptionally, it can pay to tack, for example if there is a major wind shift and the benefit gained from going about to make use of it outweighs the speed lost

Board park at a funboard regatta

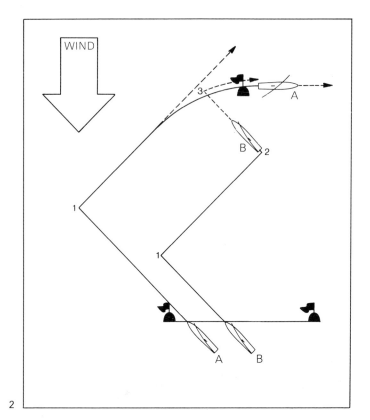

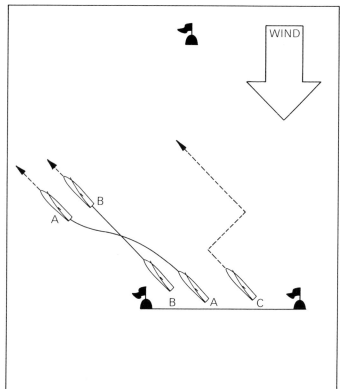

Although A overstands the mark slightly, he avoids having to go about twice

A gets his wind clear by breaking through to leeward, rather than by tacking away like C

when tacking. Given a course like that in Fig. 2, you should stay on starboard tack and if in doubt sail a few metres farther and overstand, so as to be sure of making the first mark on one tack rather than having to go about three times.

It is absolutely essential to start in the first row of boards so as to keep clear of others' dirty wind after the start, and to avoid having to tack to get a clear wind. If you are caught by a board that has got into the safe leeward position, it is often preferable to bear away and increase your speed so as to try to break through to leeward rather than to tack away from him (Fig. 3) because the increase in your speed largely compensates for the ground lost to windward.

It is also very important to be among the leaders at the first mark because the fleet will tend to spread out on the beam reach that follows. The dirty wind from boards ahead of you is so harmful that trying to break through to leeward cannot be recommended. It is better to try to work up to windward of those ahead

when the wind is lighter, so that at a suitable moment, sailing slightly freer and at greater speed, you can bear down on them and sail so close that you catch them in your own wind shadow, slowing them right down. Often they will try to defend themselves by luffing up (an effective defence when broad-reaching) but this is no help now when they are on a beam reach, and will merely slow them down still more.

Perfect mastery of gybing technique is absolutely essential if you are to be in the front of the fleet, and there are two alternative racing gybes, one long and the other short. The aim of the long gybe is to maintain board speed while turning, but the penalty is that the board sails farther because the radius of the gybe is greater. Another disadvantage is that because it takes longer to gybe that means a lengthier period of instability. The short gybe is made at full speed, but the board is braked as it turns by increasing the pressure on the stern. It is this deceleration of the board which

A beach start

accelerates the turning motion. Although the short gybe interrupts the board's speed, it takes the minimum of time and a shorter distance is covered.

Which method of gybing to use will depend on the circumstances. If you find shortly before reaching the mark that you are not the inside board, you could use the long gybe to leeward of your inside opponent with a view to having a clear wind in which to work up to windward again. The short gybe is what you will need

Euro-Funboard Cup in Sardinia
Björn Schrader, in the lead, decides on a quick
gybe because Karl Messmer and Philip Pudenz
are close on his heels: no-one is able to squeeze
between him and the mark

Jürgen Hönschied doing a power gybe

Karl Messmer gybes a long funboard

when you find you can make use of a gap which appears between the mark on one side and one or more fallen boardsailors on the other; then you will not have to sail the longer route around outside the others.

Whether the gybe is long or short, the faster it is performed the more chancy it will be, and therefore the more sure you should be that your technique is perfect.

How much risk to take also depends on the race situation at the time, for example on the position of your nearest opponent(s). If the overall points situation is such that you have nothing to lose and your only way of winning is to risk attacking, then you should take the risk. On the other hand, if you are on the defensive and have a lead over your next opponent, it would be foolish indeed to take an unnecessary risk.

Both man and material are stressed hard in funboard racing. Clothing in particular should fit well, while the board, rig, universal joint and other fittings must be checked frequently for damage, such as a worn outhaul or trapeze lines, damaged mast foot, or loose skeg box.

On the short beat (opposite page, above). In the front row, from windward, are Philip Pudenz, Robby Naish, Jürgen Hönschied, Karl Messmer

Ins and outs: short runs through the zone of breaking surf. Here Philip Pudenz leads Karl Messmer

Camden P.L.

127

Tandems

The sport of tandem windsurfing was born in 1975 when Fred Ostermann introduced his two-man board on the occasion of the Windsurfer World Championships at Bendor in France. Races were sailed between these long sailboards right from the start. Two years later over sixty competitors took part in the World Championships, and since then the Tandem Class has been recognized as International Division III, with tightly controlled parameters.

Tandem windsurfing has introduced another new dimension to the sport. Before they arrived, competition meant one person racing against another, but suddenly the opportunity came to work together as a team. Tandems are also very much faster than one-man boards in moderate winds, and it is these winds that occur most frequently. The main reason for their speed is their great length, which is however limited to 6.8 metres by the Division III regulations. Owing to the higher speed and the much greater all-up weight of the board plus its crew, there is more pressure on a tandem's sail than on that of a one-man sailboard, and this means that the sensation of 'wind' is felt much sooner on a tandem.

When racing tandems, it is not only technique but also tactics that have to be adapted to their peculiarities.

At first, the technique of tandem sailing seems easier to a novice, and with good reason because the extra length makes it more stable than, the normal single-

Sail positions when sailing closehauled, demonstrated here by Philip Pudenz and Klaus Köhnlein (G65)

Tandems bearing away on the reach

handed board. Furthermore the tandem board is more stable laterally as well as longitudinally, whether it is motionless or under way, and unlike one-man boards it is equally stable if it is a 'displacement' board, designed by using the construction rules to the extreme to produce a more dinghy-like rounded hull. While tandem sailors handle their rigs as if they were sailing a normal one-man board, the only problem which arises is that of coordination; but when tacking, gybing and manoeuvring they not only have to think about what they are doing, but to analyse and practise their moves in much the same way as the crew of a two-man dinghy communicate with each other. Teamwork and coordination can be learned easily and quickly, thanks to there being few problems over basic technique. What is more difficult is to acquire the finer technique that is required if you are to sail faster than the others.

Typical of the special technique used for tandem racing is when the two rigs are held at angles similar to those of the headsail and mainsail of a sailing boat, the object being to form a slot where the wind is accelerated between the two sails. The forward sail is set like a genoa, with the rig inclined as far aft as it can be without dipping the end of the boom beneath the surface of the water. Generally the after sail has to be raked very far forward, in light airs at least, to prevent the board from trying to luff up all the time. The nearer the sails are to each other, the closer to the wind will the tandem be able to sail, and tandem experts cross their sails even farther, with the upper third of each rig across the other. It is absolutely essential to hold the front sail as far out to leeward as possible so that airflow over the after sail is not badly disturbed, and under no circumstances should it be pulled in beyond the centreline. The sailor farther aft holds his rig as upright as he can, or may even rake it to windward to avoid the disturbed airflow from the forward sail.

It takes practice and good teamwork to master this, and it is the front man who has the more difficult job so far as technique is concerned because his rig is not balanced over the mast foot any more. For example, the sail will support itself only when airflow is attached (flowing along its length), and when it is eased out it immediately starts to fall aft. Holding the rig so far out

to leeward is also a problem. This all means that the forward sailor stands in a very awkward position, which is made particularly insecure by the turning motion of the board which is greater nearer the bow. There are considerable problems when going about and he needs practice in keeping his balance because, standing forward, he is affected by the motion of the bow as it swings sideways sharply. A jump tack is virtually impossible because, while he is in the air, the board just slips farther sideways and he lands beside it. He benefits somewhat from the fact that the sail does not have to be hardened in so far, the clew end of the wishbone being kept just beyond the edge of the board, and there is therefore less pressure on the sail, which in turn means using less energy. A further difficulty when the wind is strong is that it takes a very great deal of practice before a harness can be used.

It has been found that the closer the rigs are to each other, the better the board will perform when close-hauled, and the forward mast foot is often so close to the after mast foot that the wishbone boom of the forward rig extends beyond the after mast. This means that tacking not only involves pulling the rig parti-cularly far forward, but that the front man will find that in a crisis he is unable to save the situation by suddenly pulling back the end of the boom.

Perfect sail trim on the beat: Pudenz and Köhnlein sailing across the finish line at the European Championships

The winners of the Engadine Surfmarathon: Daniel Holinger and Karl Messmer ▷

Tandem sailing closehauled

The after position is the easier in terms of sailing technique. The man aft is positioned virtually over the boat's pivot when it turns, and he can watch the movements of the board and of the person forward, which makes it easier for him to react to changes in the trim. He needs to use more strength to control the after rig, however, because it has to be hardened in at least as far as the centreline, and is often pulled over beyond it. Furthermore, the mast often has to be raked forward, and both of these actions cause the pressure on the sail to be very high. On the other hand, it is relatively easy to use a trapeze harness.

The main difficulty in tandem sailing is steering. Because most of the people who start to sail tandems already own a one-man board, they first try to use the same method of steering, but in the case of a tandem the responsibility for luffing up and bearing away is divided between the two crew since the pivoting point, the daggerboard, lies between them. The coarsest method of steering is simply to ease out one or other sail; the board will bear away if the after sail is eased out while the front sail alone continues to draw; if it is the forward sail that is eased, the board will turn up into the wind. There is a considerable loss of speed involved when this method of steering is used, because only one sail is driving the board while it is altering direction, and for this reason the method should be used only in an exceptional situation, such as when giving way to or avoiding another board where it is necessary to also slow down.

The next alternative is to steer by raking the rig along the line of the wishbone boom, rather than exactly forward or aft in relation to the board. When the after sail is raked farther back, with the boom end thereby moved downwards, the board will be encouraged to luff up, whereas the end of the boom on the forward rig is raised to get the board to bear away from the wind. Even these rig movements are best avoided, however, first because of the risk of disturbing the airflow and second because the after rig can be backwinded by the forward rig.

The method of steering just described involves a smaller loss of speed than the first method, however, and most tandem racers soon learn the technique. But it is not the optimum because it involves having to move the rigs from the positions in which they are

Tandem sailing is fun!

normally and ideally held. The finest method of steering demands the development of great sensitivity to board speed on the part of both the crew. Any alteration of course that may be required is started as early as possible, so that the radius of the turn is large and board speed is only slightly braked. The principle is to increase or reduce pressure on both sails without altering the rake of the rig vertically. This is very demanding, technically, for the forward sailor. In order to luff up by reducing the drive of his sail he has to ease out his sail hand carefully or pull his mast hand slightly towards him, and this reduces the angle of incidence of the sail to the wind. If he wants to increase pressure in order to bear away, he has to stretch his mast hand out to leeward, and that is not so easy to do while keeping one's balance when the rig is being held in the position described earlier. The sailor near the stern uses the same technique too, but he eases out his sail hand to reduce pressure when he wants to bear away; pulling the clew to windward of the centreline to increase pressure on the sail helps the board to turn up into the wind.

It has been found that a tandem works to windward best when the board is tilted slightly to leeward, first because the edge of the board, which is immersed as part of the lateral area, is usually steeper, second because the total wetted area is reduced, and third because this puts maximum pressure on the daggerboard. As with Open Class displacement boards, a closehauled tandem performs best when it is on the limit of capsizing.

With all these methods of steering, it is the co-ordination between the two crew which is most

important of all. They have to get used to telling each other what they have noticed or observed, and to sharing ideas so that they can work smoothly together, both reacting quickly to a change in the situation.

It is particularly important to practise manoeuvring, tacking and gybing thoroughly because with a tandem board there is no conventional helmsman/crew distribution of duties; instead both sailors have an equal responsibility for board and sail handling. A tandem can be tacked as quickly as an Open Class board once the fastest of the possible techniques has been mastered. The prime mover when tacking can either be the person near the bow, or the one near the stern, depending on the type of board. When the board is round forward but has a flat planing bottom aft, the stern will swing round more readily, whereas a board that is flat forward but round aft will be turned more easily by the forward rig.

What matters most when tacking is to know beforehand what has got to be done before starting to go about. Generally the tandem tack is initiated by the sailor aft, who smoothly hardens in his rig and inclines the end of his boom downwards and back. The board is tilted rather farther to leeward with the feet to encourage it to turn into the wind. The forward sailor simply eases his sail out at the end of this phase and, when the bow is almost head-to-wind, he transfers his mast from mast hand to sail hand, 'tacks' his rig, and then hardens it in quickly with the boom pulled over beyond the centreline until the board has turned onto the new tack. When shifting his rig over to the other side, he has to rake it well forward so as to avoid catching the end of the boom on the after rig. The man aft has so far kept his rig on the original tack, pulled back well beyond the centreline, but once the forward sailor's rig is trimmed in the normal way, with the boom end over the edge of the board, the after sailor can tack his rig, preferably using a jump tack. In a moderate wind particularly, he gives the rig a final pull and can let himself land leaning out slightly to windward on the new tack, hardening in the sail with his weight. Sailing meanwhile mainly on the forward rig, the board will almost have regained its normal speed during this move, and the two rigs will be working together again as both sailors try to regain maximum closehauled speed.

On the other hand, when it is the forward crew who plays the major part, he simply waits while the board is luffing up, tacks his sail while the board is still on the old tack, and then pulls the clew right over well beyond the centreline in order to swing the bow of the board

Mylar sails

through the wind. The after rig aft is eased out early, and only hardened in after the turn when the board has taken up its new course.

Gybing a tandem also calls for close co-ordination between the two crew. In the first phase, when the board is bearing off the wind, both rigs are raked forward, with the front man holding his sail far to windward but with his mast hand rather closer so that there is lateral pressure towards what will be the new windward side. When the board is almost headed dead downwind the forward man, whose rig is now blanketed by the one behind, gybes his sail and tries to get air to flow over the new windward side of his rig, so that it can pull the bow farther to windward.

Meanwhile the man aft keeps his sail full, with the leech slightly forward, so that the turn of the stern through the wind is completed before he finally gybes his rig. The turning motion while gybing is accelerated by tilting the board steeply towards the outside of the turn.

Apart from the peculiarities of tandem sailing techniques, the ways in which tactics change also have to be considered. A tandem is considerably less manoeuvrable than one-man board, even when the crew have really mastered advanced techniques, and this has to be taken into account when preparing to start by taking up a position on the line early, and then defending it. A tandem can be sailed backwards well, but this should be the concern of the after sailor because when the front rig is hardened in the board tends to shoot stern-first into the wind. Care is also required because you lose right of way when sailing stern-first.

Congested sections of the line should be avoided if a crew is still inexperienced and not fully in control of their tandem. After getting caught in a crowd at the start it is hard to recover, and it also can often be impossible to discover who is to blame.

The best tactic is to start going at full speed, because the high laden weight of a tandem means that it is slow to gather speed. In order to get a good starting place you can, for example, try to block those to windward of you until 30 seconds before the start, while creating a gap to leeward into which you can bear away during the last few seconds to pick up speed.

After the start, it is again a question of sailing where you have a clear wind, and in view of the higher speed of a tandem it is better to work clear of another board's dirty wind by bearing away and breaking through to leeward, rather than by tacking away.

When forced to give way to an opponent on starboard tack, it is very rare (though it could happen just before reaching the finish line, for example) that going about is the right answer. It would make sense only if you could tack into the safe leeward position, but in practice it takes so long to tack that if you could gain a safe leeward position you should also be able to cross ahead of your opponent.

In most cases, the port tack board loses least if it bears away slightly in good time, because the crew can then make up for the ground lost to windward by sailing faster and crossing close astern of their opponent.

Racing courses for tandems are generally longer than for singlehanded boards. A reasonable strategy is therefore especially important for the first beat because the fleet gets well spread out, since the sides of the course can be far apart. When making for the windward mark you should get over to the right-hand side early, because you cannot tack quickly into a gap when sailing a board that's 7 metres long. If you are fairly close to the mark when you go onto starboard tack in order to lay it, you would be wise to overstand slightly so as to be on the safe side.

When reaching, it is important that the two crew should not work against each other, in other words, both sails should be similarly trimmed. A common mistake is for the forward crew to rake his rig too far forward, without noticing that the crew aft is having to harden his rig in too much so as to prevent the board from bearing away.

A tandem is particularly responsive to a change in wind speed, and the result is that board speed varies greatly. Speed is also affected when the wind blows

The forward rig is held to leeward so that the airflow over the after sail is not disturbed. Here, the three-time World Champions Pudenz and Köhnlein

from an angle nearer the bow and, when the wind is gusty, the board should therefore bear away in a gust, so as to get further to leeward, ready to luff up in the lull that follows.

Shortly before reaching the leeward mark the board should be sailed at higher speed to a position where it can be gybed, so that this has already been done before the mark is reached; it will then be free to shoot up to windward on the next leg immediately.

Tandem running downwind. The sails are held apart wing-and-wing on opposite sides to avoid creating turbulence for each other

It is even more important to have finished luffing up before reaching the leeward mark because otherwise the board will drop some considerable distance to leeward before starting the beat.

A tandem must be sailed as quietly as possible, and this is as true of the crew's movements as of their psychological state. With regard to body movement, it is a question of avoiding anything sudden. When a step has to be taken your whole body should absorb the movement, and you should put your weight onto the board toes first and then slowly lower the ball and heel of the foot. When pumping with the rigs the two crew must work in unison, with the one aft calling 'ease out – hup – back' or something similar. All commands should be given quietly so that only your partner is able to hear them. While trimming the sails your feet should always move as little as possible.

It is more important still for the crew to work together calmly if a race is to be sailed successfully. The roles that each person will play should be agreed *before* the race. Just as with a dinghy crew, winning will only come regularly if their approaches and methods are complementary. On the principle that four eyes see

better than two, each partner must inform the other of all changes in the tactical situation or wind that he has noticed. It is often easier for two people to weigh up a situation, and if each one is able to justify his opinion on some tactic a joint decision will be reached without difficulty. But it is important to share the blame for mistakes too, for an open disagreement during a race will undoubtedly cause concentration to lapse, and both sailing technique and tactics will suffer in consequence.

The fascination of speed

Speed Sailing

Speed trials have increased tremendously in number and in the interest they attract, since the invention of the sailboard. The object of the competition is to sail a certain distance as fast as possible, and this distance must be at least 500 metres if a record time is to be recognized as official by the Royal Yachting Association (RYA); a neutral observer from the RYA must also be present. Here it is not purely a question of one opponent battling directly against another: each races against the clock.

The start is flying, with the competitor taking as long a run up to the start as he wishes; the starting time is not taken until the board actually enters the timed area.

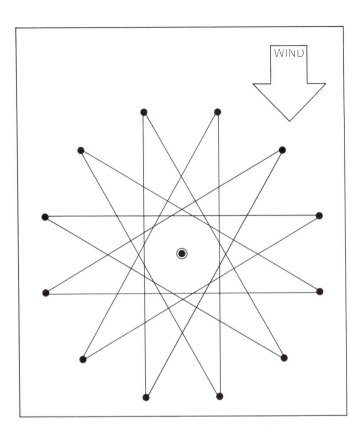

Typical speed trial course: twelve buoys, laid to mark out six lanes which can be sailed in either direction

Philip Pudenz beam-reaching

Many trials organizers lay a circle of twelve buoys which will provide six lanes or channels. This gives twelve possible courses (channels can be sailed in either direction), and an ideal course is then available whatever the wind direction. The buoys form a twelve-sided polygon, not a true circle; the diagonal of the various lanes is therefore longer than 500 metres, which means that you could sail as far as 512 metres.

This is why it is important to sail along the lane as parallel as possible to the lines between the end markers.

There are two objectives for people who take part in speed trials. First they can win the competition itself,

Ken Winner in the breakers off Hawaii

and second they can set a new record. The events, which are generally sponsored by large companies, will be organized with record-breaking in mind and will be held in the season and places where statistics show that there is a good chance of strong winds. In fact the wind must be blowing at least force $5\frac{1}{2}$ and the seas not too high for there to be any chance of setting a new record. At present the prize money for competitions of this kind is very high, and it is therefore worth considering what will happen if the wind happens to be light for it is then that equipment is most important. Anyone who intends to take part in such an event for the first time should remember that it is

A

A water start can be done with the clew held forward, by the more expert

C

B

D

Cort Larned and Philip Pudenz doing water starts and using small sails in the strong conditions

pointless to have the fastest board and the most effective sail if they are unusable, and that means basically that equipment should have been tested and practised with beforehand. Again and again competitors are seen trying out for the first time some new board or piece of gear which has only just been completed, and they frequently fail to get it to work properly at first.

When the wind is not too strong there is no problem when it comes to sailing back after having crossed measured area, and in most competitions the organizers have motor boats standing by to help, but the stronger the wind the smaller the boards become. Assistance from motor boats is then absolutely essential, because the fast boards used are 'sinkers' which have less buoyancy than is required to support the boardsailor and rig. Like water skis, sinkers are

On small boards water starts are more difficult

supported mainly by dynamic lift and, unless there is outside help available the only way to get them sailing is by doing a water start. While floating in the water with your feet touching the edge of the board, you hold the rig up above the surface and pull yourself gradually onto the board as you are lifted by the wind acting on the sail. When the wind is lighter, you have to increase the lever arm of the rig and reduce your own, by stretching up your arms while keeping the centre of gravity of your body down close to the board.

In most speed trials you can make as many runs as time allows, once the course has been declared open, but it is very rare for the principle of 'the more often the better' to be correct. Usually the wind is gusty, and there is little purpose in making a run which you do not begin going at maximum speed, or one in which you come off the plane before reaching the finish. You then take a lot of time to get back to the starting point and perhaps wait for your turn, and if the wind conditions become just right while you are returning you will be doubly unfortunate. A competitor who is used to normal racing finds it hard to adjust to the idea that only one single run matters – the fastest. The answer is to watch and wait for the right moment, which means waiting for a gust which you consider will last until you have completed your run.

As far as equipment is concerned, it is important to see that the foot of the mast and the universal joint is so fitted that the rig cannot accidentally be separated from the board, and that the footstraps stand up without twisting so that you can easily slip into them when starting. Mast sockets, daggerboard wells, skeg boxes and footstrap anchorages should have no play in them.

The skeg and the tail edge of the board must be particularly well prepared, properly filled and rubbed down smooth, and with a clean edge where flow breaks away.

As speeds of between 40 and 50 km/hr are to be expected (over 20 knots), sails should have little camber and be cut flat, especially in the forward part. It is best to have several rigs with various sizes of sail ready to use, so that you can change them as necessary. The sail should be of a size big enough that you are just able to handle it.

Speed trials are often run in the spring or autumn when it is more likely that the winds will be strong, and temperatures in Europe are low at these times of the year. It has been proved medically that there is a sharp drop in mental and physical performance when a person is cold, and adequate protection is therefore required even in 'warm' waters. Wetsuits provide good insulation and allow reasonable mobility, but there is often considerable windage owing to their shape. The ideal is to wear a suit that fits closely to the body, but has sleeves which provide enough freedom for the blood to flow, especially in your forearms.

Evening falls after a day of strenuous racing ▷▷

'Ins and Outs' and Slalom Racing

Apart from course racing, sailboards also have two other disciplines which are practically unknown in dinghy or big-boat sailing or conventional triangular course racing.

So-called '**ins and outs**' races were arranged at the Pan Am World Cup in Hawaii, which the organizer calls 'the first rough water race' ever set up. Ins and outs are short heats in small groups of a maximum of ten participants, sailed around two buoys of which one is inside and the other outside the surf or breakers. After a short upwind leg three to five circuits have to be sailed around the buoys, and a certain percentage of the group then moves up to the next round of heats.

Another possibility in strong wind conditions is starting the groups off the beach. For short funboards

without daggerboards this is a new and exciting variation, especially for the spectators.

A similar discipline is **slalom racing**, made famous in the Maui Grand Prix. The idea of the slalom is to place emphasis on two things, speed and gybing technique. There are different ways of organizing the event. One is similar to the ins and outs, with small groups racing around the course or two sailors racing side by side against each other on a parallel slalom course. In any case no upwind work is required. The group starts off from a short line and gybes through the course, which ends farther downwind. Slalom racing can be held either in waves or flat water. The heats are short and the winner(s) move up to the next round.

In 1983 and following years the European Sailboarders Association (ESA) and North American Sailboard Association (NASA) are organizing a Windsurfing World Cup and for the third time the Euro-Funboard Cup series. Every cup will consist of the three disciplines of course racing, slalom and wave-jumping.

Typical ins and outs course with three laps through the area of breaking waves

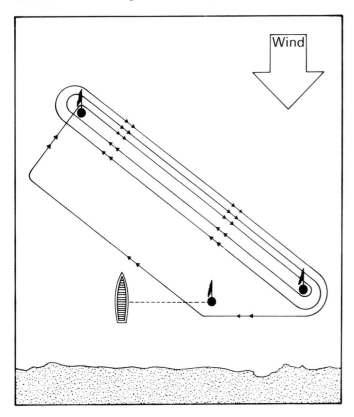

Slalom course for small groups of racers, with the finish downwind

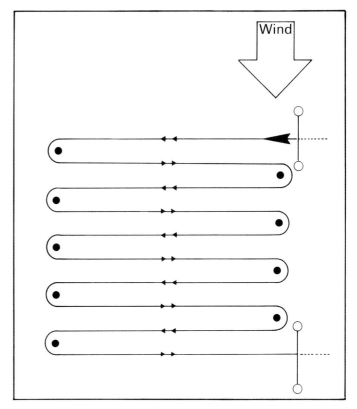

IYRU Racing Rules

IYRU YACHT RACING RULES 1981–84

Introduction

Translation and interpretation
In translating and interpreting these rules, it shall be understood that the word 'shall' is mandatory, and the words 'can' and 'may' are permissive.

Note (a) No changes are contemplated before 1985.
Note (b) These Racing Rules supersede all previous editions.

Fundamental Rules

Fair Sailing

A yacht shall compete in a race or series of races in an event only by fair sailing, superior speed and skill, and except in term races, by individual effort. However, a yacht may be disqualified under this rule only in the case of a clear-cut violation of the above principles and only when no other rule applies.

Responsibility of a Yacht

It shall be the sole responsibility of each yacht to decide whether or not to *start* or to continue to *race*.

Note *These extracts from the Racing Rules do not constitute the complete Rules, which are published in their entirety elsewhere. However, they cover some of the points which should be thoroughly understood by anyone who wants to race.*

PART I - Definitions

When a term in Part 1 is used in its defined sense it is printed in *italic* type. All preambles and definitions rank as rules.

Racing – A yacht is *racing* from her preparatory signal until she has either *finished* and cleared the finishing line and finishing marks or retired, or until the race has been *postponed, abadoned* or *cancelled*, or a general recall has been signalled, except that in match or team races, the sailing instructions may prescribe that a yacht is *racing* from any specified time before the preparatory signal.

Starting – A yacht *starts* when, after fulfilling her penalty obligations, if any, under rule 51.1 (c). (Sailing the Course), and after her starting signal, any part of her hull, crew or equipment first crosses the starting line in the direction of the course to the first *mark*.

Finishing – A yacht *finishes* when any part of her hull, or of her crew or equipment in normal position, crosses the finishing line from the direction of the course from the last *mark*, after fulfilling her penalty obligations, if any, under rule 52.2, (Touching a Mark).

Luffing – Altering course towards the wind.

Tacking – A yacht is *tacking* from the moment she is beyond head to wind until she has *borne away*, if beating to windward, to a *close-hauled* course; if not beating to windwad to the course on which her mainsail has filled.

Bearing Away – Altering course away from the wind until a yacht begins to *gybe*.

Gybing A yacht begins to *gybe* at the moment when, with the wind aft, the foot of her mainsail crosses her centre line, and completes the *gybe* when the mainsail has filled on the other *tack*.

On a Tack – A yacht is *on a tack* except when she is *tacking or gybing*. A yacht is on the tack (*starboard or port*) corresponding to her *windward* side.

Close-hauled – A yacht is *close-hauled* when sailing by the wind as close as she can lie with advantage in working to windward.

Clear Astern and Clear Ahead; Overlap – A yacht is *clear astern* of another when her hull and equipment in normal position are abaft an imaginary line projected abeam from the aftermost point of the other's hull and equipment in normal position. The other yacht is *clear ahead*. The yachts *overlap* when neither is *clear astern*; or when, although one is *clear astern*, an intervening yacht *overlaps* both of them. The terms *clear astern*, *clear ahead* and *overlap* apply to yachts on opposite *tacks* only when they are subject to rule 42, (Rounding or Passing Marks and Obstructions).

Leeward and *Windward* – The *leeward* side of a yacht is that on which she is, or when head to wind, was, carrying her mainsail. The opposite side is the *windward* side. When neither of two yachts on the same *tack* is *clear astern*, the one on the leeward side of the other is the *leeward yacht*. The other is the *windward yacht*.

Proper Course – A *proper course* is any course which a yacht might sail after the starting signal, in the absence of the other yacht or yachts affected, to *finish* as quickly as possible. The course sailed before *luffing* or *bearing away* is presumably, but not necessarily, that yacht's *proper course*. There is no *proper course* before the starting signal.

Mark – A *mark* is any object specified in the sailing instructions which a yacht must round or pass on a required side.
Every ordinary part of a *mark* ranks as part of it, including a flag, flagpole, boom or hoisted boat, but excluding ground tackle and any object either accidentally or temporarily attached to the *mark*.

Obstruction – An *obstruction* is any object, including a vessel under way, large enough to require a yacht, if more than one overall length away from it, to make a substantial alteration of course to pass on one side or the other, or any object which can be passed on one side only, including a buoy when the yacht in question cannot safely pass between it and the shoal or object which it marks.

Postponement – A *postponed* race is one which is not started at its scheduled time and which can be sailed at any time the race committee may decide.

Abandonment – An *abandoned* race is one which the race committee declares void at any time after the starting signal, and which can be re-sailed at its discretion.

Cancellation – A *cancelled* race is one which the race committee decides will not be sailed thereafter.

APPENDIX 2 - 1983
Sailboard Racing Rules

For the period 1981–1984 the IYRU will permit annual changes to Appendix 2 to be approved and implemented at each November meeting.

The following was approved in November 1982 for implementation by National Authorities at the earliest appropriate opportunity.

A sailboard is a yacht using a free sail system. A free sail system means a swivel-mounted mast not supported in a permanent position while sailing. Sailboard races shall be sailed under the International Yacht Rules modified as follows:

1 Part I – Definitions

1.1 *Leeward* and *Windward* – The side on which a sailboard is or was carrying her mainsail is assumed to be the side on which she would carry her mainsail in order to make progress forward ignoring mast heeling.

1.2 *Capsize*–
(a) A sailboard shall rank as a *capsized* yacht from the moment her masthead touches the water until her masthead is lifted from the water.
(b) A sailboard recovering from a *capsize* shall rank as a yacht which is either *tacking* or *gybing* from the moment her masthead is lifted from the water until her sail is out of the water and it has filled.

2 Part III – General Requirements

2.1 Rule 19 – Measurement or Rating Certificates
Rule 19.1 – When prescribed by the national authority a numbered and dated device on the board, daggerboard and sail shall rate as measurement certificate.

2.2 Rule 20 – Ownership of Yachts and Rule 21 – Member on Board
Rule 20.1 and 21 – When prescribed by the national authority a national class association shall be deemed to be a sailing club.

2.3 Rule 23 – Anchor
An anchor and chain or rope need not be carried.

2.4 Rule 24 – Life-Saving Equipment
Unless otherwise prescribed in the sailing instructions, a safety line shall prevent the mast separating from the hull.

2.5 Rule 25 – Class Emblems, National Letters and Sail Numbers

Rule 25.1(a) – The class emblem may be displayed once on each side of the sail. It shall fit within a rectangle of 0.5m², the longest dimension of which shall not exceed one metre. It shall not refer to anything other than the manufacturer or class and shall not consist of more than two letters or numbers. When approved by the IYRU or a national authority within its jurisdiction, this emblem is not considered advertising.

Rule 25.1(c) – A sailboard shall carry on her sail a sail number allotted either to the board or to its owner. This number shall be issued by a national authority or its duly authorised body.

2.6 Rule 26 – Advertisements and Sponsorship

Rule 26.1(a)(ii) – One builder's mark may be placed on the hull and shall fit within a rectangle of 0.5m².

Rule 26.1(a)(iii) – The sailboard's type may be displayed on the hull in two places. The letters shall not exceed 20cm in height.

Rule 26.1 add a new paragraph (c) – One manufacturer's mark, of the board, its equipment or clothing, may be displayed on each item of clothing worn by a competitor, provided that it fits within a square not exceeding 10cm × 10cm, except as provided under rule 26.2 (Sponsorship).

3 Part IV – Right of Way Rules

3.1 Rule 38.2 – Same Tack – Luffing and Sailing Above a Proper Course after Starting

Rule 40 – Same Tack – Luffing before Starting

The normal station of the helmsman shall be at the aft edge of the centreboard well. For 'mainmast' read 'mast foot'.

3.2 Capsized when Starting

Between her preparatory and starting signals a sailboard shall have her sail out of the water and in a normal position, except when *capsized*. She shall have the onus of satisfying the race committee that a *capsize* was unintentional and that every effort was made to recover immediately.

3.3 Sailing Backward when Starting

When approaching the starting line to *start* or when returning to the pre-start side of the starting line a sailboard sailing or drifting backward shall keep clear of other sailboards or yachts which are *starting* or have *started* correctly.

4 Part V – Other Sailing Rules

Rule 60.1 – Means of Propulsion

Dragging a foot in the water infringes this rule.

5 Part VI – Protests, Penalties and Appeals

Rule 68 – Protests by Yachts

A sailboard shall not be required to display a flag in order to signify a *protest* as required by rule 68.2, but, except when rule 68.3 applies, she shall notify the other sailboard or yacht by hail at the first reasonable opportunity and the race committee as soon as possible after *finishing* or retiring.

6 Appendix 3 – Alternative Penalties for an Infringement of a Rule of Part IV

6.1 720° Turns

Two full 360° turns of the board shall satisfy the provisions of the 720° turns penalty. When prescribed in the Sailing Instructions, a greater penalty may be imposed by increasing the number of turns.

7 Rules for Multi-Mast Sailboards

7.1 The mainsail is the foremost sail and the mainmast is the foremost mast.

7.2 Rule 1.2(a) – A sailboard shall rank as a *capsized* yacht from the moment all her mastheads touch the water until one masthead is lifted from the water.

7.3 Rule 1.2(b) – A sailboard recovering from a *capsize* shall rank as a yacht which is either *tacking* or *gybing* from the moment one masthead is lifted from the water until all her sails are out of the water and they have filled.

7.4 Rule 3.1 – The normal station of the helmsman is the normal station of the crew member controlling the mainsail.

7.5 Rule 3.2 – for 'sail' read 'sails'.

Reproduction of these extracts from the Racing Rules and of the complete text of Appendix 2, the Sailboard Racing Rules (1983) is by kind permission of the International Yacht Racing Union, 60 Knightsbridge, London SW1, U.K.

IYRU Construction Rules

Rules for the International Division I of Sailboards

1 General

1.1 The International Division I of Sailboards has been established by IYRU to enable 'flat' boards to compete together on a reasonably equal basis.

1.2 The International Authority for the International Division I of Sailboards shall be the IYRU.

1.3 Interpretations of these Rules shall be made by the IYRU.

2 Administration

2.1 *Language*

2.1.1

The official language of the Division is English and in the event of a dispute over interpretation the English text shall prevail.

2.1.2

The word 'shall' is mandatory and the word 'may' is permissive.

2.2 *Eligibility*

2.2.1

A sailboard is not permitted to race in the Division unless:
(i) it is an International Mistral, Windglider or Windsurfer, in which case Rule 3.2 does not apply, or
(ii) it has been measured and found to comply with these Rules, or
(iii) it is in a class approved by the IYRU or the relevant National Authority as being eligible to compete in the Division.

2.2.2

The National Authority may prescribe that:
Either: Each sailboard competing in the Division shall have a current IYRU Division I 'sticker' permanently attached to it.
Or: The competitor shall hold a current Surfer-Pass.

2.2.3

The IYRU and the National Authoriry reserve the right to withdraw recognition of a class even if it complies with the specific requirements of these Rules.

2.2.4

It is the owner's responsibility to ensure that his sailboard spars, sails and equipment comply with these Rules at all times.

2.3 *IYRU Measurement Instructions*

Except where other methods of measurement are specifically indicated all measurements shall be carried out in accordance with the IYRU Measurement Instructions.

2.4 *Identification Marks*

2.4.1

The board and sail shall have permanent and clearly marked numbers.

2.4.2

The sail shall carry the National Letter(s), National Number and the sailboard insignia, if it has one, in accordance with the IYRU Racing Rules. The minimum size of sail letters and numbers shall be:

Height	225mm
Width	150mm (excluding number 1 and letter I)
Thickness	30mm
Spacing	45mm

3 Construction and Measurement Rules

3.1 *Materials*

Any materials may be used except that carbon fibre, Kevlar and high-modulus fibres or exotic materials are prohibited.

3.2 *Board*

3.2.1

The overall length shall not exceed 3900mm. If the towing eye, required by Rule 3.2.11, is a separate fitting attached to the board the overall length, including such fitting, shall not exceed 3920mm.

3.2.2

In these Rules 'the fair deck line' refers to the fore-and-aft line of the deck at its highest point in transverse section, disregarding any local variation. This line need not be on the centreline of the board.

3.2.3

In the Rules 'the fair underside' refers to the fore-and-aft line of the hull at its lowest point in transverse section, disregarding any local variations. The fair underside need not be on the centreline.

3.2.4

The width at the widest point of the board (measured at half height) shall be 630mm minimum and 700mm maximum.

3.2.5

The beam measured at a height of 50mm above the fair underside shall be not less than 590mm over a length of 1750mm, the forward end of which shall be not more than 1200mm behind the bow.

3.2.6

The maximum depth of the board measured from the fair deck line to the fair underside shall not exceed 165mm anywhere on its length.

3.2.7

There shall be no visible air gap dividing the board longitudinally throughout its length when afloat in an upright sailing position fully equipped but without crew.

3.2.8

The beam measured at a height of 22mm above the fair underside shall be not less than 450mm, except within 800mm of the bow and within 100mm of the stern.

3.2.9

The board shall incorporate not less than 0.1 cubic metre (100 litres) of closed-cell foam plastic or the same volume of expanded polystyrene blocks.

3.2.10

The weight of the board with skeg(s) but without centreboard and mast step or other equipment shall be not less than 18kg when in a clean and dry state.

3.2.11

A towing eye shall be fitted to the board not more than 200mm from the bow.

3.2.12

There shall be an attachment for a mast leash.

3.2.13

Any board may be disallowed on grounds of safety if the hull has any sharp upwards projecting edges of radius less than 15mm.

3.2.14

The board shall have a minimum volume of 200 litres.

3.3 Centreboard or daggerboard

3.3.1

The depth of the centreboard shall not exceed 700mm measured normal to the fair underside of the board.

3.3.2

The centreboard shall be capable of insertion into the board from its upper side and shall have stops to prevent it exceeding the depth in Rule 3.3.1.

3.3.3

Remote methods of centreboard adjustment by control lines or any other means are prohibited

3.4 Skeg(s)

3.4.1

Not more than two skegs shall be fitted.

3.4.2

The depth of the skeg(s) shall not exceed 300mm measured normal to the fair underside of the board.

3.4.3

If two skegs are fitted they shall be an equal distance and a maximum of 700mm from the stern.

3.4.4

Remote methods of skeg adjustment by control lines or any other means are prohibited and the skeg(s) shall not project above the deck.

3.5 Mast

3.5.1

The length of the mast shall not exceed 4700mm measured from the deck at the mast foot; the measurement shall include any local raising of the deck which has the effect of increasing mast height.

3.5.2

At any cross-section normal to the mast's axis, the mast shall be circular and of uniform wall thickness. The bending curve shall be equal in every direction. Tapering of the mast is allowed. Pre-bent masts are prohibited.

3.5.3

The construction of the joint and downhaul fitting between the mast and board is optional but it shall be possible to incline the mast to an angle of at least 90° to the vertical in every direction unless the sheer of the deck prevents this.

3.5.4

The mast shall be capable of release from the board by a sharp upwards pull.

3.6 Boom

The size of the boom is optional.

3.7 Fittings and Control Lines

3.7.1

Any fittings, such as blocks and cleats for the control of the rig, shall be directly attached only to the mast or boom.

3.7.2
The layout and type of control lines is optional, except as limited by 3.7.1.

3.7.3
There shall be no lines and fittings acting to control the mast bend other than the outhaul, kicker (boom vang) or topping lift.

3.7.4
Harness attachments may be fitted to the boom and may be adjustable.

3.7.5
The mast shall have a safety line attached to the board to prevent the mast parting from the board if the mast step releases. This safety attachment shall have a breaking strain of not less than 50kg.

3.8 *Sail*

3.8.1
The sail shall be made in accordance with the requirements of the IYRU Measurement Instructions except that:
(a) reinforcement having the effect of stiffening the sail shall not extend more than 400mm from the head and the tack (measured from the aft side of the mast sleeve) and at the clew (measured from the clew measurement point);
(b) the use of Mylar or other non-woven materials in any form is prohibited;
(c) window size is limited as rule 3.8.8.

3.8.2
These rules are for a triangular sail, in which the mast pocket forms part of the sail. The mast pocket shall not exceed 150mm in width as shown in the diagram and shall extend downwards to the tack measurement point or beyond.

3.8.3
The tack of the sail shall be at the point on the forward edge of the mast pocket which is opposite to the point at which the foot or its extension intersects the rear edge of the mast pocket, and where the line between these two points is at right angles to the forward edge of the mast pocket. See diagram.

3.8.4
The clew shall be at a point at which the foot or its extension intersects the leech or its extension.

3.8.5
The head shall be at a point on the forward edge of the mast pocket which is opposite to the point at which the leech intersects the rear edge of the mast pocket, and where the line joining these two points is at right angles to the forward edge of the mast pocket. If the intersection point of the leech and mast pocket is not clear, the head is found by a perpendicular measurement of 150mm from the forward edge of the mast pocket to the leech. See diagram.

3.8.6
The sail dimensions shall be a maximum of:

Luff	AE	4400
Leech	AG	4300
Head to midfoot	AF	4300
3/4 height width	BK	940
1/2 height width	CJ	1680
1/4 height width	DH	2270
Foot	EG	2580

as shown on the sail diagram.

3.8.7
The half points on the luff, leech and foot shall be found by folding the head to the tack, head to the clew and clew to the tack respectively. The quarter and three-quarter points shall be found by folding the head, tack and clew to the half points on the luff and leech.

3.8.8
The total area of the transparent part of the sail window(s) shall be a minimum of 0.4m² and a maximum of 1m². The window(s) shall not be placed closer to the luff, leech or foot than 150mm.

3.8.9
There shall be a maximum of three batten pockets on the leech.
(a) In the case of three pockets they shall be positioned so that their centrelines are not more than 100mm from the leech measurement points.
(b) In the case of two the upper shall not be higher than the three-quarter height, the lower shall not be higher than the half height.
(c) In the case of one pocket it shall not be higher than the three-quarter height.

3.8.10
The length of the batten pockets shall not exceed:

Three pockets		Two pockets		One pocket
Top	375mm	Upper	375mm	375mm
Middle	725mm	Lower	725mm	
Lower	525mm			

And their width shall not exceed 40mm.

3.8.11
Lines in the leech and/or foot of the sail are prohibited, except that a non-adjustable leech line may be used to reinforce the leech of a sail without batten pockets.

3.8.12
Only one attachment point may be fitted at the tack and only one attachment point may be fitted at the clew. An additional attachment point may be fitted to the leech for reefing at a minimum of 300mm from the clew eye. One attachment point may be fitted at the head. No other attachment points shall be allowed on the leech or foot of the sail.

3.8.13

Headboards are prohibited.

3.8.14

Sails shall carry the identification marks required by Rule 2.4.2. Any sail maker's mark shall be within 385mm of the tack, which for the purposes of this Rule shall be taken as the intersection of the aft side of the mast pocket and the foot of the sail.

4   Foot Straps

Foot straps are prohibited.

5   Crew

The crew shall be one person.

6   Limitation of Equipment

6.1

During a race meeting only one board, two sails and two centreboards may be used. The board shall not be altered in any way during the race meeting. Only one sail and only one centreboard shall be carried during a race. Other equipment is interchangeable so long as it complies with these Rules.

6.2

A harness is permitted.

6.3

Wind indicators and telltales are permitted.

6.4

A compass is prohibited.

6.5

A weight jacket is prohibited.

7   Weight Groups

It is recommended that there are two weight groups. The lightweight group maximum should be below 75kg crew body weight and the heavyweight group minimum should be above 70kg crew body weight.

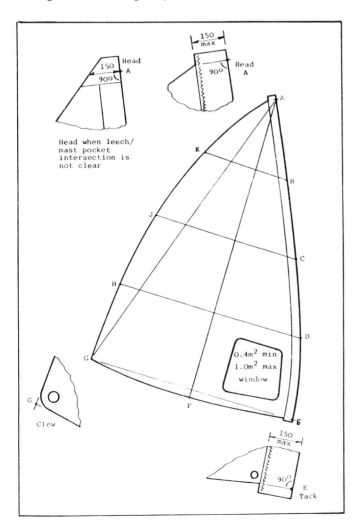

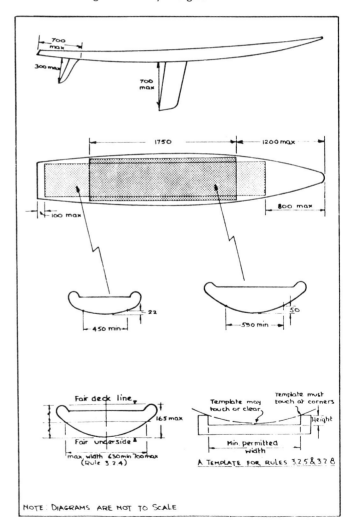

Rules for the International Division II of Sailboards

1 General

1.1 Division II of the International Division of Sailboards shall be a singlehanded development class.

1.2 The International Authority for the International Division II of Sailboards shall be the IYRU.

1.3 Interpretations of these Rules shall be made by the IYRU which may consult the International Board Sailing Association (IYRU Division II) (IBSA).

1.4 No liability or legal responsibility in respect of these Rules can be accepted by the IYRU or its delegated representatives.

2 Administration

2.1 Language

2.1.1
The official language of the Division is English and in the event of a dispute over interpretation the English text shall prevail.

2.1.2
The word 'shall' is mandatory and the word 'may' is permissive.

2.2 National Authority

In countries where there is no National Authority (NA) or in which the NA does not wish to undertake the administration of Division II of the International Divisions of Sailboards, its functions as stated in these Rules shall be carried out by the 'National' Board Sailing Association which is recognized by the IBSA.

2.3 Eligibility to Race

2.3.1
No sailboard shall race in Division II unless it complies with the current Rules.

2.3.2
It is the owner's responsibility to ensure that his sailboard complies with the Rules at all times and that alterations or replacements to the sailboard do not contravene the Rules.

2.4 Measurement

2.4.1
Only a measurer officially recognized by the National Authority or the National Board Sailing Association (IYRU Division II) of the country in which the measurement is undertaken shall measure a sailboard, its mast, sail and equipment. If no such bodies exist the IBSA may appoint a measurer.

2.4.2
The measurer shall report to the IBSA and the NA anything which he may consider to depart from the intended nature of the Division II Sailboard, or to be against the interests of the sport and in this event notwithstanding anything in these Rules, the IBSA or NA may refuse to let a sailboard race.

2.4.3
All sailboards shall be liable to measurement checks by the recognized measurer at the discretion of the IBSA, the NA or the race committee at any time.

2.5 IYRU Measurement Instructions

2.5.1
Except where other methods of measurement are specifically indicated, all measurements shall be carried out in accordance with the current IYRU Measurement Instructions.

2.5.2
All measurements shall be in metric units.

2.6 Identification Marks

2.6.1
The NA shall issue sail numbers which shall be consecutive and the numbers shall be preceded by the National Letter(s). It shall be the responsibility of each NA, or the appropriate national Board Sailing Association (Division II), to furnish IBSA regularly with a list of sail numbers issued.

2.6.2
The sail shall carry the National letter(s), National Number and the sailboard's insignia, if it has one, in accordance with IYRU Racing RUles. The minimum size of sail letters and numbers shall be:

Height	225mm
Width	145mm (excluding number 1 and letter I)
Thickness	30mm
Spacing	45mm

2.6.3
The sail shall carry the Division II insignia above the boom height in the proximity of the clew. The insignia shall be as indicated in the diagram.

2.6.4
The Division insignia may be carried on the starboard side of the sail only.

2.6.5
All insignia, letters and numbers shall be of a durable material, of a colour contrasting with the sail, and shall be securely attached.

3 Construction and Measurement Rules

3.1 Materials

Any materials may be used except that carbon fibre, Kevlar and other high-modulus fibres, and exotic materials are prohibited.

3.2 Board

3.2.1

The overall length shall not exceed 3900mm. If the towing eye, required by Rule 3.2.10, is a separate fitting attached to the board the overall length, including such fitting, shall not exceed 3920mm.

3.2.2

In these Rules 'the fair deck line' refers to the fore-and-aft line of the deck at its highest point in transverse section, disregarding any local variation. This line need not be on the centreline of the board.

3.2.3

In the Rules 'the fair underside' refers to the fore-and-aft line of the hull at its lowest point in transverse section, disregarding any local variations. The fair underside need not be on the centreline.

3.2.4

The minimum width shall be 630mm at the widest point of the board measured at half height between the fair deck line and the fair underside; unless the widest point of the board is below the half when width is measured at the widest point.

3.2.5

A minimum depth of the board measured from the fair deck line to the fair underside shall not exceed 220mm anywhere on its length.

3.2.7

There shall be no visible air gap dividing the board longitudinally throughout its length when afloat in an upright sailing position fully equipped but without crew.

3.2.8

(a) The board shall contain not less than 0.1m³ of closed-cell foam plastic or the same volume of expanded polystyrene blocks.

(b) The measurer may require board owners to insert up to two inspection bungs in the hull in such a way that the internal foam may be checked.

3.2.9

The weight of the board with skeg(s) but without centreboard or other equipment shall be a minimum of 18kg when in a clean and dry state.

3.2.10

A towing eye and a mast leash attachment shall be fitted to the board. The towing eye shall be capable of supporting a minimum of 50kg suspended from it. The mast leash is governed by 3.7.5.

3.2.11

Any board may be disallowed on grounds of safety if the hull has any sharp upwards projecting edges of radius less than 15mm.

3.2.12

Footstraps on the board are prohibited.

3.3 Centreboard

3.3.1

The depth of the centreboard shall not exceed 700mm measured normal to the fair underside of the board.

3.3.2

The centreboard shall be capable of insertion into the board from its upperside and shall have stops to prevent its length exceeding that of 3.3.1.

3.3.3

Remote methods of centreboard adjustment by control lines or any other means are prohibited.

3.4 Skeg(s)

3.4.1

The depth of the skeg(s) shall not exceed 300mm measured normal to the fair underside of the board.

3.4.2

If two skegs are fitted then they shall be an equal distance and a maximum of 700mm from the stern.

3.4.3

Remote methods of skeg adjustment by control lines or any other means are prohibited and the skeg(s) shall not project above the deck.

3.5 Mast

3.5.1

The length of the mast shall not exceed 4700mm measured from the deck at the mast foot; the measurement shall include any local raising of the deck which has the effect of increasing mast height.

3.5.2

At any cross-section normal to the mast's axis, the mast shall be circular and of uniform wall thickness. The bending curve shall be equal in every direction. A tapering of the mast is allowed. Pre-bent masts are prohibited.

3.5.3

The construction of the joint and downhaul fitting between the mast and board is optional but it shall be possible to incline the mast at an angle of at least 90° to the vertical in every direction unless the sheer of the deck prevents this.

3.5.4

The mast shall be capable of release from the board by a sharp upwards pull.

3.6 Boom

The size of the boom is optional.

3.7 Fittings and Control Lines

3.7.1
Any fittings, such as blocks and cleats for the control of the rig, shall be directly attached only to the mast or boom.

3.7.2
The layout and type of control lines is optional, except as limited by 3.7.1.

3.7.3
There shall be no lines and fittings acting to control the mast bend other than the outhaul, kicker (boom vang) or topping lift.

3.7.4
Harness attachments may be fitted to the boom and may be adjustable.

3.7.5
The mast shall have a safety line attached to the board to prevent the mast parting from the board if the mast step releases. This safety attachment shall have a breaking strain of not less than 50kg.

3.8 Sail

3.8.1
Sails shall be made in accordance with the requirements of the IYRU Measurement Instructions except that:
(a) reinforcement having the effect of stiffening the sail shall not extend more than 400mm from the head and tack (measured from the aft side of the mast sleeve) and at the clew (measured from the clew measurement point);
(b) the use of non-woven material (such as Mylar) in any form is prohibited;
(c) window size shall be limited as Rule 3.8.8.

3.8.2
These Rules are for a triangular sail, in which the mast pocket forms part of the sail. The mast pocket shall not exceed 150mm in width as shown in the diagram and shall extend downwards to the tack measurement point or beyond.

3.8.3
The tack of the sail shall be at a point on the forward edge of the mast pocket which is opposite to the point at which the foot or its extension intersects the rear edge of the mast pocket, and where the line between these two points is at right angles to the forward edge of the mast pocket. See diagram.

3.8.4
The clew shall be at a point at which the foot or its extension intersects the leech or its extension.

3.8.5
The head shall be at a point on the forward edge of the mast pocket which is opposite to the point at which the leech intersects the rear edge of the mast pocket, and where the line joining these two points is at right angles to the forward

pocket is not clear, the head is found by a perpendicular measurement of 150mm from the forward edge of the mast pocket to the leech. See diagram.

3.8.6
The sail dimensions shall be a maximum of:

Luff	AE	4400
Leech	AG	4300
Head to mid-foot	AF	4300
3/4 height width	BK	940
1/2 height width	CJ	1680
1/4 height width	DH	2270
Foot	EG	2580

as shown on the sail diagram.

3.8.7
The half points on the luff, leech and foot shall be found by folding the head to the tack, head to the clew and clew to the tack respectively. The quarter and three-quarter points shall be found by folding the head, tack and clew to the half points on the luff and leech.

3.8.8
The total area of the transparent part of the sail window(s) shall be a minimum of $0.4m^2$ and a maximum of $1m^2$. The window(s) shall not be placed closer to the luff, leech or foot than 150mm.

3.8.9
There shall be a maximum of three batten pockets on the leech.
(a) In the case of three pockets they shall be positioned so that their centrelines are not more than 100mm from the leech measurement points.
(b) In the case of two the upper shall not be higher than the three-quarter height, the lower shall not be higher than the half height.
(c) In the case of one pocket it shall not be higher than the three-quarter height.

3.8.10
The length of the batten pockets shall not exceed:

Three pockets		Two pockets		One pocket
Top	375mm	Upper	375mm	375mm
Middle	725mm	Lower	725mm	
Lower	525mm			

and their width shall not exceed 40mm.

3.8.11
Lines on the leech and/or foot of the sail are prohibited, except that a non-adjustable leech line may be used to reinforce the leech of a sail without batten pockets.

3.8.12
Only one attachment point may be fitted at the tack and only one attachment point may be fitted at the clew. An additional attachment point may be fitted to the leech for reefing at a minimum of 300mm from the clew eye. One attachment point may be fitted at the head. No other

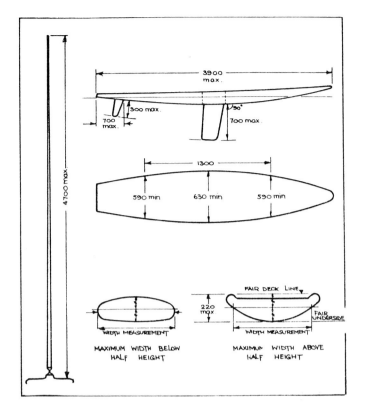

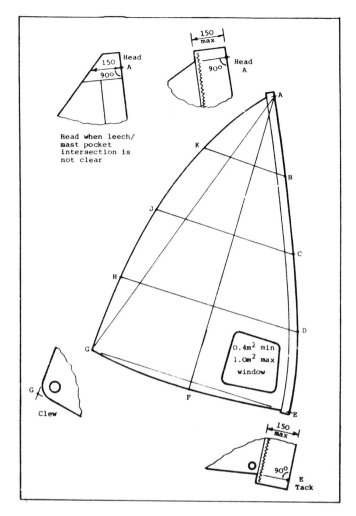

attachment points shall be allowed on the leech or foot of the sail.

3.8.13

Headboards are prohibited.

3.8.14

Sails shall carry the identification marks required by Rule 2.6. Any sail maker's mark shall be within 385mm of the tack, which for the purposes of this Rule shall be taken as the intersection of the aft side of the mast pocket and the foot of the sail.

4   Crew

The crew shall be one person.

5   Limitation of Equipment

5.1

During the race meeting only one board, two sails and two centreboards may be used. The board shall not be altered in any way during the race meeting. Only one sail and only one centreboard shall be carried during a race. Other equipment is interchangeable so long as it complies with these Rules.

5.2

A harness is permitted.

5.3

Wind indicators and telltales are permitted.

5.4

A compass is prohibited.

5.5

A weight jacket is prohibited.

6   Racing Rules

Racing will take place under IYRU Yacht Racing Rules as modified by the Appendix for Board Sailing.

7   Weight Groups

It is recommended that there are two weight groups. The lightweight group maximum should be below 75kg body weight and the heavyweight group minimum should be above 70kg crew body weight.

Rules for the International Division III of Sailboards

1 General

1.1 The International Division III of Sailboards has been established to enable tandem sailboards of different designs, but complying with these Rules, to compete together.

1.2 The International Authority for the International Divisions of Sailboards shall be the IYRU.

1.3 Interpretations of these Rules shall be made by the IYRU which may consult the International Tandem Class Association (ITCA).

1.4 No liability or legal responsibility in respect of these Rules can be accepted by the IYRU or its delegated representatives.

2 Administration

2.1 Language

2.1.1
The official language of the Division is English and in the event of a dispute over interpretation the English text shall prevail.

2.1.2
The word 'shall' is mandatory and the word 'may' is permissive.

2.2 Authority

2.2.1
In the countries where there is no National Authority (NA) or the NA does not wish to administer the Division, its functions as stated in these Division Rules shall be carried out by the recognized Tandem Class Association or its delegated representative.

2.3 Certificate

2.3.1
Every sailboard entering a race shall hold a valid certificate in accordance with IYRU Racing Rule 19.

2.3.2
A sailboard holding a certificate of a class recognized as being within the Division, and which complies with its class rules, shall be deemed to have a certificate in Division III.

2.3.3
Notwithstanding anything in these Rules the IYRU or NA shall have the power to refuse to grant a certificate to, or to withdraw a certificate from, any sailboard.

2.3.4
It is the owner's responsibility to maintain his sailboard in accordance with these Rules.

2.4 Measurement

2.4.1
Only a measurer officially recognized by the National Authority or the recognized class association of the country in which the measurement is undertaken shall measure a sailboard, its masts, sails and equipment. If no such bodies exist the ITCA may appoint a measurer.

2.4.2
The measurer shall report to the NA and to the ITCA anything which he considers to depart from the intended nature of the Division III Sailboard, or to be against the interests of the sport. In this event, notwithstanding anything in these Rules, the NA may refuse to issue a certificate.

2.4.3
All sailboards, masts, sails and equipment shall be liable for remeasurement at the discretion of the NA or race committee.

2.5 Measurement Instructions

2.5.1
All measurement shall be carried out in accordance with the current IYRU Measurement Instructions, except where other methods of measurement are specifically indicated.

2.6 Identificiation Marks

2.6.1
In accordance with Racing Rule 25 every sailboard shall carry a letter or letters showing her nationality and a sail number and may carry a class emblem.

2.6.2
Sail numbers shall be issued consecutively.

2.6.3
The letters and numbers shall be placed in accordance with Racing Rule 25 on the forward sail. The size of letters and numbers shall be not less than:

Height	225mm
Width	145mm (excluding number 1 and letter I)
Thickness	30mm
Spacing	45mm

2.6.4
All emblems, letters and numbers shall be of a durable material, be clearly visible while racing and shall be displayed on the forward sail. If the aft sail carries letters or numbers they shall be the same as those displayed on the forward sail, unless the sailing instructions prescribe otherwise.

2.6.5
The board shall be clearly identified by a serial number on the board which shall be entered on the certificate.

3 Construction and Measurement Rules

3.1 *Materials*

Any materials may be used except that fibres such as Kevlar and other high-modulus or exotic materials are prohibited. However, carbon fibre is permitted to be used, in the board only.

3.2 *Board*

3.2.1

The overall length shall not exceed 6800mm.

3.2.2

In these Rules 'the fair deck line' refers to the fore-and-aft line of the deck at its highest point in the transverse section, disregarding any local variation. This line need not be on the centreline of the board.

3.2.3

In these Rules 'fair underside' refers to the fore-and-aft line of the hull at its lowest point in transverse section disregarding any local variation. The fair underside need not be on the centreline of the board.

3.2.4

The width of the board at half height between the fair deck line and the fair underside shall be not less than 650mm and not more than 750mm at its widest point. If the widest point of the board is below half height then the width is measured at the widest point.

3.2.5

The width measured at height of 30mm from the fair underside of the board shall not be less than 500mm over a length of 4560mm, the forward end of which shall be not more than 700mm from the front of the board.

The width measured at height of 50mm from the fair underside of the board shall not be less than 600mm over a length of 3950mm, the forward end of which shall be not more than 1200mm from the front of the board.

3.2.6

The maximum depth of the board measured from the fair deck line to fair underside shall not exceed 250mm anywhere on its length.

3.2.7

If the cross-section of the board has a concavity in its underside, when the board is afloat and upright, but without mast, booms and sails, at its lowest point the concavity shall be completely below the waterline.

3.2.8

The weight of the board with skeg(s) but without centreboard or other equipment shall be not less than 50kg when in a clean and dry state.

3.2.9

A towing eye and mast leash attachments shall be fitted to the board. The towing eye shall be capable of supporting a minimum of 100kg suspended from it. The mast leashes are governed by 3.7.4.

3.2.10

A board may be disallowed on grounds of safety if the hull has any sharp upward projecting edges of radius less than 15mm.

3.2.11

The board shall contain not less than 0.2m³ of closed-cell foam plastic or the same volume of expanded polystrene blocks.

3.3 *Centreboard*

3.3.1

The depth of the centreboard shall not exceed 910mm measured normal to the fair underside of the board.

3.3.2

The centreboard shall be capable of insertion into the board from its upper side and shall have stops to prevent its depth exceeding that specified in Rule 3.3.1.

3.3.3

Remote methods of centreboard adjustment by control lines or fittings, or any other means, are prohibited.

3.3.4

The maximum width of the centreboard shall not exceed 270mm. Its maximum thickness shall not exceed 25mm.

3.4 *Skeg(s)*

3.4.1

The depth of the skeg(s) shall not exceed 300mm measured normal to the fair underside of the board.

3.4.2

Remote methods of skeg adjustment by control lines or any other means are prohibited and the skeg shall not project above the deck.

3.5 *Mast*

3.5.1

The length of the mast shall not exceed 4700mm measured from the fair deck line at the mast top.

3.5.2

At any cross-section normal to the axis of the mast the mast shall be circular and of uniform wall thickness. The bending curve shall be equal in every direction. A tapering of the mast is allowed. Pre-bent masts are prohibited.

3.5.3

The construction of the joint and downhaul fitting between the mast and the board is optional but it shall be possible to incline the mast to an angle of at least 90° to the vertical in every direction unless the sheer of the deck prevents this.

3.5.4

The mast shall be capable of release from the board by a sharp upwards pull.

3.6 Boom
The size of the boom is optional.

3.7 Fittings and Control Lines

3.7.1
Any fittings, such as blocks and cleats for the control of the rig, shall be directly attached only to the mast or boom.

3.7.2
The layout and type of control lines is optional, except as limited by 3.7.1.

3.7.3
There shall be no lines and fittings acting to control the mast bend other than the outhaul, kicker (boom vang) or topping lift.

3.7.4
Each mast shall have a safety line attached to the board to prevent the mast parting from the board if the mast step releases. This safety attachment shall have a breaking strain not less than 50kg.

3.8 Sail
3.8.1
Sails shall be made in accordance with the requirement of the IYRU Measurement Instructions except that:
(a) Reinforcement having the effect of stiffening the sail shall not extend more than 400mm from the head and the tack (measured from the aft side of the mast sleeve) and at the clew (measured from the clew measurement point).
(b) Window size shall be limited as in Rule 3.8.8.

3.8.2
These Rules are for triangular sails, in which the mast pocket forms part of the sail. The mast pocket shall not exceed 150mm in width as shown in the diagram and shall extend downwards to the tack measurement point or beyond.

3.8.3
The tack of the sail shall be the point on the forward edge of the mast pocket which is opposite to the point at which the foot or its extension intersects the rear edge of the mast pocket, and where the line between these two points is at right angles to the forward edge of the mast pocket. See diagram.

3.8.4
The clew shall be at a point at which the foot or its extension intersects the leech or its extension.

3.8.5
The head shall be at a point on the forward edge of the mast pocket which is opposite to the point at which the leech intersects the rear edge of the mast pocket, and where the line joining these two points is at right angles to the forward edge of the mast pocket. If the intersection point of the leech and mast pocket is not clear, the head is found by a perpendicular measurement of 150mm from the forward edge of the mast pocket to the leech. See diagram.

3.8.6
The sail dimensions shall not exceed:

Luff	AE	4400mm
Leech	AG	4300mm
Head of mid-foot	AF	4300mm
3/4 height width	BK	940mm
1/2 height width	CJ	1680mm
1/4 height width	DH	2270mm
Foot	EG	2580mm

as shown in the sail diagram.

3.8.7
The half points on the luff, leech and foot shall be found by folding the head to the tack, head to the clew and clew to the tack respectively. The quarter and three-quarter points shall be found by folding the head, tack and clew to the half points on the luff and leech.

3.8.8
The total area of the transparent part of the sail window(s) shall be a minimum of $0.4m^2$ and a maximum of $1m^2$. The window(s) shall not be placed closer to the luff, leech or foot than 150mm.

3.8.9
There shall be a maximum of three batten pockets on the leech.
(a) If there are three pockets they shall be positioned so that their centrelines are not more than 100mm from the leech measurement points.
(b) If there are two the upper shall not be higher than the three-quarter height, the lower shall not be higher than the half height.
(c) If there is one pocket it shall not be higher than the three-quarter height.

3.8.10
The length of the batten pockets shall not exceed:

Three pockets		Two pockets		One pocket
Top	350mm	Upper	700mm	700mm
Middle	700mm	Lower	500mm	
Lower	500mm			

and their width shall not exceed 40mm.

3.8.11
Lines in the leech and/or foot of the sail are prohibited, except a non-adjustable leech line may be used to reinforce the leech of a sail without batten pockets.

3.8.12
Only one attachment point may be fitted at the tack and only one attachment point may be fitted at the clew. An additional attachment may be fitted to the leech for reefing at a minimum of 300mm from the clew eye. If the tack cringle is in the mast sleeve and comprises a cringle in each side of the sleeve, and functions as one cringle, they shall be considered to be one cringle. No other attachment points shall be allowed on the leech or foot of the sail.

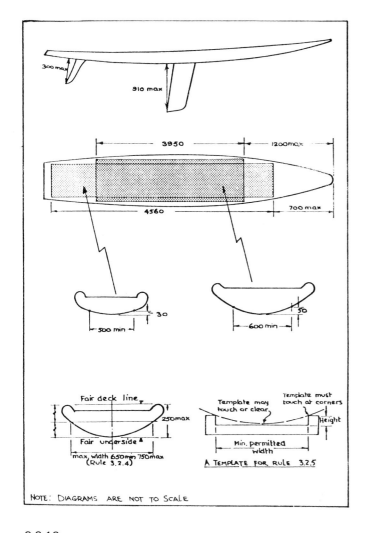

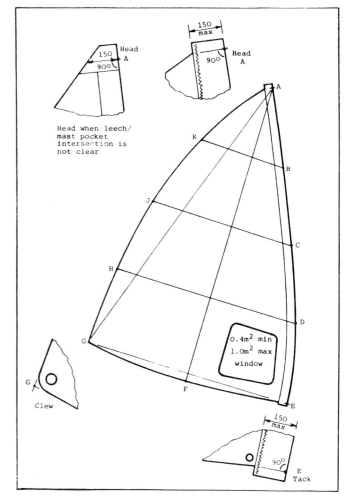

3.8.13
Headboards are prohibited.

3.8.14
Sails shall carry the identification marks required by Rule 2.6. Any sail maker's mark shall be within 515mm of the tack measurement point.

3.9 *Limitation of Equipment*

3.9.1
During the race meeting only one board, four sails and one centreboard may be used. The board shall not be altered in any way during the race meeting. Only two sails shall be carried during the race. Other equipment is interchangeable so long as it complies with these Rules.

3.9.2
Harness(es) is(are) permitted.

3.9.3
Wind indicators and talltales are permitted.

3.9.4
A compass is prohibited.

These Division Rules will be effective until December 31, 1984. Any amendments to be incorporated into them will be agreed in November 1983.

Reproduction of the International Rules for Division I, II and III Sailboards is by kind permission of the International Yacht Racing Union, 60 Knightsbridge, London SW1, U.K.